'KICKED INTO TOUCH'

Fred Eyre

...... is not only an autobiography, but an object lesson to all aspiring young footballers that life is not all about Wembley Stadium and England Caps.

Fred Eyre's experiences in the lower regions of the game are both witty and enlightening.

His life story illustrates that the world doesn't come to an end if a youngster is released by a top league club. His success in the cutthroat world of big business, where he built an empire from a humble capital outlay of £150, is proof of what can be achieved with a little foresight, a lot of courage and hard work and a touch of good fortune.

"The harder I worked the luckier I seemed to get"!!

He speaks with the confidence of a man who has experienced almost everything in football — Groundstaff Boy — Apprentice Professional (Manchester City's first ever) — Full-Time Professional — Part-Time Professional — Non-Contract Player — Player/Manager — Youth Team Manager — Reserve Team Manager — Scout — Assistant Manager — Manager of Fourth Division Wigan Athletic. Over a thousand games played at various levels in a career spanning 22 years, 46 games played in twenty-one countries around the world complete a formidable background.

He played for 20 clubs in 20 years! Played under 29 Managers and 82 Coaches!

His fund of anecdotes and stories make unusual, interesting and humorous reading.

ISBN 1 872127 00 2

Printed and Bound in Great Britain by
Woolnough Bookbinding, Irthlingborough
Northamptonshire

CONTENTS

LIST OF ILLUSTRATIONS

Following page 112

Photographs by courtesy of:

The Bolton Evening News
The Manchester Evening News
The Lincolnshire Echo
Mr Brian Simpson

The Lancashire Evening Post
My Dad's Brownie box camera!!

Cover by:
Les Williamson
County Press

INTRODUCTION

After refusing numerous requests to write my autobiography, due to the fact that I was acutely aware that hardly anybody knew who I was, I finally dismissed this unusual display of modesty and set about the task.

Overlooking the sea in Cannes, the warm January sunshine inspiring me, whilst Britain shivered back home, appealed to my sense of the unusual as a particularly apt place for a 'Blackley Boy' from a North Manchester council estate to begin to recount his early life.

I was warned that it wouldn't be an easy job, but I found it relatively simple writing about my favourite subject ..... ! My thanks go to my previous 112 Managers and Coaches! without whom it wouldn't have been possible for me to compile this book, to Manchester City whose free transfer set me on the road to stardom! to my Mother and Father, who have supported me all my life, and to my wife Judith, who inherited the debris and helped me pick up the pieces.

My thanks to Lynn and Susan for their efforts with the typewriter and to Jack Edgar for persuading me to write this masterpiece!

one

THE END
or as it turned out –
the beginning

Manchester City 'A' team versus Bury 'A', not really a fixture to remember; it would be, I thought, a similar game to hundreds of games I'd played in before. How wrong I was, it was to be a very significant day for me.

The routine had been the same that Saturday as it had always been, up about 9 am, just a cup of coffee for my breakfast, a walk to the local shops, a five-minute walk away on Charlestown Road, in Blackley, a working-class suburb in North Manchester where I lived, to get the boiled ham for our Sunday tea the next day.

I always did this for my mother on Saturdays, you had to be there early to get the best of the ham! She did the main shopping herself later.

The neighbours would call across as I strolled through our council estate "Are you playing today Son ..... Good Luck", or just simply "All the best today". I was the local boy who was on his way to the top. I was surrounded by people who wanted me to succeed, good people, Blackley people, and for me there was nowhere like Clough Top Road where I lived. I loved Clough Top Road and most of the people in it.

We lived in a cul-de-sac, off a big street—it had four houses on each side all joined together—which opened out on to one of Manchester's biggest parks, Boggart Hole Clough. I lived there with my Mam and Dad and it was a measure of how closely knit we all were by the fact that I always called the neighbours on our side Auntie this and Uncle that instead of the usual Mister and Missus.

Blackley was a sprawling council estate where families had gone to live prior to and during the war, and they were all good, honest, decent people, the only type of people I knew.

I had trampled through their gardens so many times that my ginger hair passing their windows to retrieve my ball, when it hadn't done what my feet wanted it to, had become a way of life to them, as indeed it was for me.

The 'ham mission' accomplished successfully, I then nipped next door but one to Collinge's, the local newsagents, for my supply of 'Beech Nut' chewing gum. No other brand would do, it had to be 'Beech Nut'. Before my first game for my school team many years previously somebody slipped me a piece and I played well, so a packet of 'Beech Nut' was an essential part of my equipment from then on. Indeed there have been occasions when the supply has run out and I have begun to panic as I scoured the neighbourhood for an alternative supplier of the stuff.

On one occasion I simply could not manage to obtain any, so I settled for the more expensive 'Wrigley's' and had a grueller of a game that afternoon, and I was convinced that the 'Wrigley's' was to blame!

However, I was in luck that day; and with the 'Magic Gum' safely in my pocket was soon on my way back home, a couple of more ''Good Lucks'' ringing in my ears. Up until now a fairly normal and satisfactory morning.

My routine with the gum was to pop a piece into my mouth just as we kicked off and keep it until I gave a bad pass, then I would spit it out. But I abandoned this habit because by the end of the game the taste had gone!! ..... if only it were true.

Back home I packed my gear, had my usual piece of toast and coffee and was ready to go, my carriage was waiting ..... in its terminus, the number 88 bus from St. John Boscoe's, the usual 'thumbs up' sign from my Mother at the door as I left, and I was away, a quick change of bus in Newton Street, off one bus and on to the number 76 to complete my journey to Maine Road.

I knew the timetables of the buses better than I knew my two times tables. I had been crossing the city of Manchester this way every day since the age of eleven when I passed my eleven plus to Ducie Avenue, which was a mere corner kick away from Maine Road, so the big City held no fears for me.

It was mid-day and as usual on the day of the big match, even at this relatively early hour, there was a buzz about the place that would make the hairs stand up on the back of my neck; I just couldn't wait for it to be my turn!!

..... But for today I was still an 'A' team lad battling for stardom and I boarded our Finglands coach for the short journey to Urmston, City's training ground in Chassen Road, with the rest of the boys for the encounter with Bury.

On the coach journey, after a few laughs and a joke with my team mates, I settled down on the front seat with a young boy aged about seven or eight to keep him company. He was a polite lad, very well mannered and looked well scrubbed with his tanned cheeks glowing. He looked very smart in his school blazer with matching school cap and grey short pants.

He was a nice little boy and I liked him and used to enjoy our little chats about football whenever he accompanied the team.

Twenty years later whenever I see him I still enjoy our little chats about football but these days he can speak with a little more authority, having been transferred to Leeds United for a record £350,000 transfer fee from Blackpool, and Paul Hart became one of the best centre halves in England.

His Dad, Johnny, was one of my heroes. When I was a young boy I used to cheer him on from my position behind the goal at the scoreboard end and I admired his goalscoring ability and also his bravery. Now he was a team mate of mine. He was almost at the end of his career and his job was to help us youngsters along.

Just before we reached the ground we always stopped the coach at a local cafe 'The Hughenden' to pick up the cakes and pies for both teams to devour at the end of the game, and it was young Paul's job to nip off the coach and bring the pies back quickly whilst the coach held up all the traffic on the High Street.

Finally we were there and the coach drew up at the familiar dirt track leading to the ground. It was neatly kept, with flood-lights. The pitch was usually in good nick, the sun was shining, there was a spring nip in the air and all seemed to be going to plan as I grabbed my favourite peg to change before anybody else claimed it and upset my routine; no problems so far I thought.

Soon we were all changed and ready for action, the team talk took its usual course, Johnny mumbling a few instructions, Dick Niellson banging his right fist into his left palm to indicate that he expected us to give them a bit of stick. Good old Dick .... he was like a Father to me ..... he should be, I'd been stuck in his team for so long that I'd known him for almost as long as my Father!

"Be positive for the crosses," he would tell the keeper. "Mark them tight," were the instructions to the full-backs, and so on through the entire team, but never anything to me. He used to just toss me the ball before I led out the team with the instructions "Keep 'em going".

I used to take his lack of communication as a compliment, vainly and stupidly thinking I must be doing everything cor-rectly; that I had nothing else to learn because they had nothing else to tell me and that it was just a matter of time before I made the first team.

City at that time were rich in talent for wing halves, which was my position, but I cared little for their reputation, because I thought I was making progress, slow progress, but progress nevertheless.

Ken Barnes had been a great player, "The best uncapped wing half in the Country" was the title bestowed on him by the sportswriters. It was not a title I would have liked. The best capped wing half would have suited me better. Ken had been a City regular for years, since joining the club from non League Stafford Rangers, and was a vital member of the team which reached Wembley two years running, and it was he and Don

Revie who were the key figures in the famous 'Revie Plan' which revolutionised soccer.

But Ken had come to the end of his illustrious career and had joined Wrexham, so that would make more room for me!

His expensive replacement, a record £45,000 signing from Scotland, Bobby Kennedy was having trouble finding his form and was being switched to full-back in an attempt to help him settle down to life in the English First Division.

Alan Oakes, a fine young player, was making the other wing-half spot his own with some sterling performances and his consistency was to give him a club record of appearances before he eventually left the club.

Former Manchester Schoolboys stars Dave Shawcross and Roy Cheetham were challenging each other for the other wing-half spot, but they were recovering from serious injury and illness respectively so they also had their problems.

There was my team mate, Graham Chadwick, who although we were in the same team was a couple of years older than me.

Then there was a young whippersnapper called Mike Doyle who was coming along on the blind side. He had already caused me a minor problem on his very first day at the club by getting involved in a scrap with winger Bobby McAlinden, which resulted in me being called before the Manager to receive a good dressing down for 'allowing it to happen' as a senior player, whilst the two culprits got off scot free. British justice!!!

Finally, there was John Benson. On my first appearance for City four years previously I was obviously quite nervous, but I was put at my ease and helped through the game by the inside forward playing in front of me.

This was John Benson, a stocky kid a couple of years older than me, who although he seemed to be struggling a bit himself (at his age he should have been in a higher team than the fifth team) still took time to assist me. I've never forgotten this and have liked him ever since.

A couple of seasons later, however, he proved to be a big headache as he was switched from a struggling inside forward to a fine wing half to provide even more competition for these precious places.

I was far from happy about his switch, but was too frightened of the Manager to go and see what it was all about; my opportunity to investigate the situation came as I boarded the number 60 bus outside Baxendale's to go home one day after training.

There was only one seat available on the bus and I grabbed it. I needed a seat to rest my legs after a rigourous day's training, and I was surprised to see the other occupant of the seat was Harry Godwin, the scout who had signed me for the club.

Here was the chance to get the problem of John Benson off my chest. "We've decided he won't make it as an inside forward so we are just trying him in another position for his swan song," were Harry's exact words. I didn't know what this meant, but it sounded promising.

Twenty years later he was still at the club as assistant manager .....some swan song!

Good luck to him; anyone that helps me, I'm glad when they do well.

So while these lads had problems of their own to solve, I would step in, claim my place in the first team and go on to gain a record number of caps for England!

Such thoughts were going to change rapidly in the next 65 minutes. "All the best lads," I shouted over my shoulder to the crocodile of sky blue shirts filing out of the dressing-room door behind me. "Yeah! all the best Fred," three or four shouted back and we were off, out of the door, studs clinking down the concrete, still one of my favourite sounds even to this day, especially if my feet are inside them! to be met by a roar of indifference from our handful of loyal supporters. Local Urmston pensioners most of them, who loved their football but preferred the simple pleasures of Urmston to the hurly-burly of First Division grounds, with the added bonus of saying to their mates in the pub over a Guinness whenever one of us hit the big time "I saw him when he was a kid of sixteen in the 'A' team, knew he was a good 'un the first time I set eyes on him."

In view of the clement weather the crowd was touching 30 that day, not thousand ..... just about 30, I'm not sure because one of them moved whilst I was counting and before I could commence a recount the whistle had blown to start the game.

There was never any crowd trouble in those games because usually the players outnumbered the spectators! It was the usual Bury type of game, hard and dour, it's strange how they used to follow the same pattern against Bury, but usually we managed to win in the end.

Just after half-time with the score 1-1 the ball broke loose around the centre circle between the City number four and the Bury number five. The odds were in favour of the big strapping Bury defender as he moved in to tackle. However, the much lighter City wing half decided to go for it as well, and due to the fact that he was over stretching, met the ball badly balanced with no weight behind his leg at exactly the same time as his beefy, perfectly balanced opponent.

The twangs could be heard streets away, it sounded like a guitar instrumental as every ligament that I knew I possessed snapped plus a few that I didn't know I had.

I lay there, and for a minute I couldn't believe it. My ankle, my knee, I couldn't decide which was the worst as I lay there waiting for the stretcher.

I began to get things into perspective as I lay amongst the muddy boots, sky blue socks, white socks, knobbly knees, cut knees, scarred knees as they stood around me ..... waiting, this was my worm's eye view as I lay there ..... waiting.

"Is it broke?" one player asked another. "Oh no," I thought, I hadn't considered the possibility of the dreaded break, the one injury all players fear most.

"No, it's ligaments this," said the other.

"Thank God," I thought, lulled into a false sense of security for a second.

"They are much worse than a break."

"Bloody Hell," I thought, as we waited .....

In the end somebody had the presence of mind to enquire "Where is that damn stretcher? The lad's dying here."

At last a human being!

I heard an old voice shout from the dressing-room door, "We can't find it".

I thought it was about time I took a hand in the proceedings and dictated my own destiny. So hoisting myself up onto my elbow, the pain now unbelievable, I informed them that it was outside propping up the dressing-room wall at the back amongst the dandelions and overgrown grass where no man had trodden for at least ten seasons.

Finally it arrived, rusted from the top to bottom due to its exposure to the elements all those years.

Bugs were crawling along the metal frame and as I was lifted onto it my hands sank into two cobwebs as I gripped the sides, ready to be hoisted up and away.

There was much grunting and groaning as the old volunteers made their way with me to the sanctuary of the dressing-room. My view of things was as before, a superb view up two pairs of nostrils and the sight of their faces going redder and redder. The only thought in my mind was "I hope they don't drop me".

Polite applause reached my ears as we neared the touch-line, one die-hard squeezed my arm and told me not to worry.

Soon I was enveloped in the confines of our dressing-room, the smell of linament lingered in the air as I lay there, contemplating both my future and how I was going to get dressed.

The Bury number 5 Spike Rawlinson went on later in life to become a professional comedian starring in the night clubs of his native North-East, but he certainly did not make me laugh that day.

Little did I know that this unglamorous and undignified exit was to be the end of me at Manchester City, my last appearance in my beloved sky blue shirt; all my dreams, my one single-minded aim in life would end that day, because a few weeks later an official looking envelope dropped through the letter-box of 30 Clough Top Road informing me that I had been given a free transfer.

So my career at City ended at exactly the same place as it had started ..... Chassen Road, Urmston.

two

ON THE SCRAP HEAP

I was now in a predicament that I had not envisaged. This situation definitely was not included in my plans, discarded at nineteen and struggling to even walk let alone impress another club enough for them to consider offering me a contract.

I thought at the time that the injury had influenced the club's decision. I now realise that this was not so, the writing had been on the wall for me for many months previously only i had been too blind to see it.

One seldom lingers long enough to read one's own graffiti and this had been the case with me. I had missed the tell-tale little signs, like the Boss telling me we were playing Newcastle away when really it was Stoke at home! When they started wrapping my boots in a road map I really should have cottoned on, but no, City was my team and although the last few months had been heart breaking at times, I still had the single-minded thought that I would come through.

There were times regularly when trainer Jim Meadows, another of my former heroes (I was in tears as he was carried off in the 1955 Cup Final defeat by Newcastle United with an injury that finished his career), would announce that there would be a practice game and gather the whole playing staff together on the pitch and proceed to announce the two teams, handing out shirts to the first team and then announcing the reserve team, who would be providing the opposition. As each name was called he would grab a shirt and trot off ready for the game.

When this was completed I was the only person left standing there, not knowing what to do, because not a word was said to me; if I stayed where I was the game would have to be played around me!

I thought this was a particularly hard way to treat a young player and it happened on a few occasions, but even as I left the scene to go and knock a ball about in the gym by myself I still could not see that even then I was on my way out.

Oh! the folly of youth.

I never imagined that such feelings of despair could ever be attached to the game of football when I first decided that I would make it my career ..... at the tender age of three.

My Dad took me along to Maine Road ..... where else? to see the legendary Frank Swift, at that time the world's best goalkeeper; 'Big Swifty', always the entertainer, always playing to the crowd, but always a great keeper. He was later to be tragically killed in the Munich air crash in 1958 when the fabulous Manchester United 'Busby Babes' team was decimated.

This day, however, he was facing the mighty Arsenal. The red shirts with white sleeves were swarming all over City and 'Swifty' was a busy man keeping them at bay. Bert Sproston was playing at full-back with a knee bandage on to support a 'dicky' knee and these were the two who held my attention as the Gunners beat City 0-3.

I decided there and then that this was the life for me and come what may I must one day wear that sky blue shirt.

With this thought always on my mind to spur me on, I set about kicking my ball in our back garden with much more gusto; already I had an aim in life.

Soon my birthday arrived and my joy knew no bounds when, as I hurriedly ripped open my present, I discovered a green goalkeeper's jersey just like 'Swifty's'. They didn't have sophisticated sports shops in those days like they do today and my Mother had worked a miracle in converting an old boy scout's jersey into my goalkeeper's ensemble, but that didn't matter to me, I never had it off my back.

Soon I was to start school. My parents encouraged me to go because they said they had organised class football matches there and I began classes at the very tiny St Mary's school in Moston. This was the only school that could take me, but it was a very small school and from the start my parents tried to get me into a bigger one. There weren't even enough boys to form a football team, so obviously it wouldn't do! My Mother and I were walking about four miles a day to get there and back.

So I was transferred, not for a big fee, to Crosslee School, Victoria Avenue, in Blackley, where on the very first day there was a class football match in the afternoon.

I could hardly wait because I knew I was good at football and even though I didn't know anybody's name I was confident that when I had knocked in a few goals that afternoon I would soon be popular with everybody.

Came the great event and I never got one single kick of the ball. It was whizzed about at great speed by kids who knew each other, had grown up together, and the whole thing just passed me by. A kid called Victor Boff dominated the whole game, scored goals at will, and at the end of the day it was an astonished shell-shocked little seven-year-old who was met by his Mother at three-thirty.

I had to wait a whole week, till the same time the following week, for my next game, a week in which the three 'R's' were forgotten as I planned to do considerably better this time round.

It was, after all, only a class game, but for me a Wembley Cup Final couldn't have been more important as I mentally prepared myself for the encounter that day.

Thankfully, things went much better as I got into the game from the off and literally dribbled myself stupid as I took on opponent after opponent to rattle in a few goals.

The match was watched by Mr Ellison, who unknown to me also picked the school team, but he was always in the company of the giants of the fourth year so meant little to me at the time.

Friday at 3 pm was always a big day at Crosslee. The whole school would gather in the hall and Miss Stone, our lovable, kind-hearted, but slightly eccentric head mistress would take the stage and make all the school announcements. This was followed by a deathly hush as she announced like a judge pronouncing the death sentence the names of the children who that week had received an 'order mark'. This was the ultimate in disgrace at Crosslee and anybody who received one would be avoided and pointed at for weeks after as though he or she was a leper.

After this came the school football team fixture. This Friday she announced that they would be playing tomorrow at home against 'Christ The King' and as each boy's name was called out he had to go onto the stage to ceremoniously receive his shirt. The green shirt of Crosslee was one prize I longed for, but it was a long way away yet because the team were all eleven-year-olds and with me barely just seven, four years seemed a long time to wait.

She went through the entire team and then said "The reserve for tomorrow is Fred Eyre". There was a gasp from the hall as about 500 heads and 1,000 eyes swivelled and focused on me. I couldn't believe my young ears, I got to my feet and made my way shakily up onto the stage to receive my reserve shirt. It felt like gold to me, though actually it was a red one. For some reason the reserve got a red one; maybe it made you appreciate it more when you progressed to the actual team and got a green one.

The applause was still ringing in my ears as I flew out of the school gate and ran all the way home. As kids straggled home I could hear them say "That's the kid who is reserve for the school team tomorrow, he's only a first year". My feet barely touched the ground as I pelted my way home through the prefabs of Colmore Drive. When I got home I insisted that I put it on "just to get the feel of it" and run across Blackley to my Grandma's in Belthorne Avenue to show her. It seemed a little big, but when I tied up the neck where there were holes with string through, it didn't flap around too much and anyway I didn't care what it looked like as I went to bed that night hoping that at least one of the players wouldn't turn up next day. Manchester City, I'm on my way!

So the great day dawned and my dream came true, the centre half did not turn up and after a brief consultation with skipper Barry Skinner, secretly my latest hero—if only I can be as good as him when I get older—it was decided to slot me straight in at centre half. Even to my young years I thought that a rather strange decision because centre halves were usually the biggest lads who could kick the ball further than anybody else, not little ball players who were four years younger and two foot smaller and two stone lighter than everybody else on the field.

Still, I didn't care, I was going to play, that was the main thing, and I had my number one fan, my Mother, standing shivering on the touchline to give me confidence.

I must have stood out like a sore thumb as we lined up for the kick-off, in my red shirt, whilst the rest of my team mates wore green, and my tensions were not eased when, whilst waiting for the referee to start the game, one of our opponents spotted me and shouted to his centre forward, my immediate opponent, "Hey have you seen the size of that young kid, when you get near him cart him".

I didn't exactly know what the phrase "cart him" meant, but realised instinctively that it meant something unpleasant.

Still "get stuck in and hope for the best" was my thought for the day as we roared to a memorable 4-0 victory. I was over-joyed and was never left out of the team again as I went on to play for a record four years.

Nothing can stop me now!

three
ON MY "SWEENEY" TODD AT DUCIE

My years at Crosslee flew by, I'd been very happy there but now it was time for the eleven-plus examination which would determine where I would be spending the next five years of my life. I was one of those borderline cases and had to take the thing again before finally passing. I had the choice between Ardwick Tech. or Ducie Avenue. Both were a long way from my home, so I made a few discreet enquiries amongst my friends which school had the better football team and that was how I ended up at Ducie.

It was a decision I never regretted even though the school was set in one of the less salubrious areas of Manchester, in Denmark Road, in the heart of Moss Side, where even the Alsatians roamed about in pairs!

It was a big school with a good reputation. Lord Robens was a former pupil, and my parents were pleased that I was going there but were a little apprehensive of the long journey morning and night.

My Dad took the morning off that first day, which proves it was a day of great importance in the Eyre household because never in my eleven years on earth did I remember my Dad taking any time off work. I had many illnesses in my childhood but my Dad used to go on and on, never missing a day.

He worked as a butcher for Mr Smalley, a family butchers with one shop in Rochdale Road, in Collyhurst, and the other, which my Dad ran single-handed, just off Bradford Road in Ancoats.

We were not a rich family by any means but Dad worked hard to make sure we were never short of anything, least of all football boots for me.

It was to this shop every Saturday from the age of three my Mother would take me on three buses, deposit me at the shop and take three buses back again in order that my Dad could take me for my weekly dose of football.

City one week, United the next, we never missed a match. We would stand in the same spot amongst the same group of people every week and I would be passed down to the front over everybody's heads to lean on the wall perched on a specially made box so I could see over, protected by these massive adults cheering my favourites.

How times have changed. It was a wonderful experience for me to be amongst healthy, vigorous men simply cheering on their team, none of the obscene chants that you hear today and never a hint of violence.

Only once in all my years standing behind those goals at the scoreboard end (actually just to the right of the goals, because I was tipped off by a stalwart supporter very early on, ''Don't stand right behind the goals son, the players look like chips in a chip pan'') did I see any violence.

That was on a day when City's big Dave Ewing and Everton's Dave Hickson were having a rare old battle and an Evertonian got a bit carried away and hit somebody with his rattle. He was soon ejected from the scene but such was the rarity of the misdemeanour that it was talked about for seasons to come.

Even at this tender age, I'd seen all the greats, obtained their autographs; I simply lived for weekends.

Each Saturday a big match and each Sunday I would board the coach to watch my local team, White Moss Villa, play in the pub league all over Manchester; maybe if it wasn't City then it could be White Moss Villa when I grew up ..... No! unthinkable, it had to be City.

Our green Austin 7 drew up outside the big iron gates of

Ducie Avenue. I put my new leather school bag over my shoulders—it was my prize for passing the exam—and prepared to venture into the unknown. I smoothed down my brand new blazer, looked proudly at my new badge, a giant bee, straightened my school cap and set forth. A very tiny boy was just walking in at the same time and his small stature made me feel a little bolder; we both took deep breaths and marched in together.

I had hoped to see him at dinner time, an ally to spend the hour with, but I couldn't see him anywhere and I was amusing myself by dribbling a stone about on a quiet stretch of playground. I was nicely balanced, head bowed over the ball just like Roy Clarke dashing down the left wing at Maine Road, when all of a sudden a great shadow was cast over me—I thought it was night-time already: I glanced up, thinking "I'll stick it through his legs before scoring". Sixty thousand people were just waiting for me to tap the stone into an empty net after a dribble that had taken me past fourteen defenders— the first four I'd beaten had recovered and come back for a second beating—to score City's winning goal in the last minute and now my way to goal had been blocked by this gorilla! Instead I found myself staring into the stomach of a giant sixth-former, a glance to the right and I saw another, a swift glance to the left and there was another, and I didn't need to look behind to know there were another two behind me.

I raised my sights a little higher to find myself looking into the far from pretty face of John Thaw, perhaps he was already rehearsing for some of the tough guy roles he would portray in films and on TV like 'The Sweeney' in the future.

His face was grim, a huge mole just over one eye, camouflaged by many a clever make-up man since then, magnetised my attention.

"Hey fag," he spat out the words through tight lips. All first years were called 'fag' so I didn't mind, not that I had much choice in the matter! "Go to the tuck shop and get me a packet of Durex."

I looked in the direction of the tuck shop and saw a quaint, matronly lady selling penny Arrowbars, Trebor chews, Milky lunches but nothing marked 'Durex'. I hesitated a second then Wham! a dozen pennies wrapped in a handkerchief can prove to be a formidable weapon when crashed down onto the back of your head, it can also serve as a sharp reminder not to hesitate when Mr Thaw wanted something doing.

Now I hadn't a clue what a packet of Durex was, but I knew you didn't chew them and I was pretty sure you didn't smoke them, but I knew I was going to have to go and ask for them, so I slowly held out by hand for the money, my brain working over-time because I knew I was in a tricky situation. Fingering the bump that was slowly coming up on the back of my head, I made my way to the tuck shop. I could see Wagon wheels galore, Mars bars, everything but these damned things. I decided to hang about inside the shop for a short while before dejectedly coming out of the shop shaking my head. The least I'll get I thought is another couple of whacks with the pennies. ''She says she has sold out,'' I announced, inwardly grimacing at the thought of what was to come, but I was in for a pleasant surprise as the five of them turned on their heels roaring with laughter in search of another victim.

I was grateful for my narrow escape but my head was thumping after being hit by the pennies. The 'change' didn't do me any good that day, but the experience did.

"Wonder what that prick wants a packet of Durex for anyway?"

four

DUCIE BITS TO SAVOUR

Ducie Avenue was in my opinion a fine school. The headmaster Mr Hughes, known affectionately to everybody as "Sam", was first class, dignified but caring and most of the teachers were the same.

The main feature as far as I was concerned, however, was the fact that it didn't just have one school football team, but three.

The under 12's for the boys in the first and second year, the under 14's for those in the third and fourth year and the under 16's for the big lads.

Came the first football day, the teacher gathered us all together and said "It's not often anyone gets in the school team in the first year but those who fancy their chances can stay for trials". I was there like a shot and we were all sorted out into positions. Unknown to us, the school team had already virtually been picked from last year's boys but anyone who impressed might just sneak in. There were two of us for the centre forward spot and as I might have guessed the teacher told the other lad to play there, so I made a dive for the right wing as my second choice.

I took an immediate dislike to the teacher from that moment. "He couldn't pick the winner in a one horse race," I thought as we lined up for the kick-off. As the whistle blew, the aspiring centre forward set off directly down the centre of the field punting the ball in front of him whilst everybody just stood and watched him in amazement, the teacher blew the whistle and shouted to him "You have to pass it to somebody from a kick-off, son". I stared in disbelief, here was I the future Captain of England, stuck out on the right wing while the donkey that had taken my place doesn't even know the rules. "Sorry, Sir," he replied as we lined up again. This time he promptly turned round and booted the ball back to our own startled goalkeeper.

"What have I let myself in for here?" The ball was brought back and I quickly volunteered to exchange places with him in order to actually set the game in progress. Then we finally got started. The game had been going precisely two minutes when I picked up a pass just inside my own half, beat two or three players and shot just wide of the post. "Oh, shit!" I muttered under my breath, really disappointed at my effort, an early goal would have done me a power of good.

"Stop the game, come here Eyre," the teacher beckoned me. His hearing must be uncanny, I thought, he was at least 50 yards away and I barely uttered the offending words; he's going to send me off, expel me from the school. The colour drained from my face. "What will my Dad say?" I slowly trudged across to him and his beckoning finger. "That's enough for you, go and join in the other game and have a trial for the under 14's team."

What a superb teacher he was, what a shrewd judge of talent! My earlier dislike for him evaporated as my face changed back to its normal colour. I trotted over to the other game. This teacher looked at me, obviously thinking this little eleven-year-old had come with some message or other. "Mr Mitchell says I've to join in this trial, Sir," I announced proudly. "Oh really, he thinks you are up to it does he?" he said rather patronisingly. I didn't really need an extra spur, but I remember thinking "Just let me get on and I'll wipe that smirk off your face".

"Where do you want to play?" he asked. I'd been studying things a bit whilst I'd been waiting on the touchline and these were really big lads compared to me, so whilst I really fancied my usual centre forward job I thought I'd be safer out of the way a bit and I said "Outside right please, Sir" and then I was on.

It was a great feeling playing with lads who could really play; when they hit a ball it usually went where they intended it to go. I was on their wavelength and I liked it.

It took me a minute or two to realise the difference. The left winger got down the line and hammered over a cross to where really I should have been, but I was so used to wingers' crosses not reaching the far post that I never bothered taking up the correct position. I vowed there and then that the next time that winger got clear and put a cross in I would be on the end of it.

Shortly after this he broke free again and I galloped in as fast as my legs could carry me; over came the cross, over and over it soared, clearing everybody's heads as I tried to go even faster to get there to meet it. My head connected just right as I flew horizontally through the air, the ball sailed past the keeper's outstretched hands into the goal. The feeling cannot be described as I was helped to my feet by my new team mates.

As a result of the game I was in this team as well. A month later the big lads began their fixtures and to cap it all I got a game in that team as well. I was going to be a busy boy. It was a good job each team didn't play on the same Saturday or I could have been in trouble. If I kept my place in every team I would be able to represent the school non-stop for the next five years. What a good school this is, it's only the maths, geography etc. that spoils it.

I did in fact play for the next five years, and through all the teams my particular team never lost one single game.

We had a fantastic side, totally unbeatable, although we did once get one scare when Heald Place held us to a 2-2 draw and a lad called Neil Young caused us a few problems. This was the first time I came across Neil, but in later years our paths were to cross many times and he became a very close friend and colleague at City.

Three of us gained Manchester area honours and later on as we got older Bobby Smith and Dave Latham, both later to sign for Manchester United, joined us in the trials for the full Manchester Boys team. Five boys from one school—it took some beating.

five

THE KING OF BOGGART HOLE CLOUGH

Every spare minute at home was spent playing in Boggart Hole Clough.

Boggart ..... Hole ..... Clough, I love the very sound of the name. Until many years later, when I went to Disneyland in America, for me it was THE number one spot in the world—when you've only been as far as Blackpool you are easily pleased!

I knew every blade of grass, every tree personally by name.

It derived its name because many years ago a Boggart was reported to live there—a Boggart is another name for a ghost. This may be true, but the only ghosts I ever saw were ones wearing sky blue shirts in my mind's eye. Ghosts of the past great players, as I played and played, practised and practised on the hockey pitch, with coats down for goals.

As soon as I was home from school, and all day Sunday, it was down to the Clough; all the school holidays (it never seemed to rain in those days) were spent in this vast woodland. People always knew where to find me and apart from the pitches there was a lake to run around, a proper running track, quite a thing in those days, many hills to climb and 'The Hollows'—big crevices with trees of all shapes and sizes to climb—and at the bottom a fairly deep, muddy, stagnant stream, full of rubbish, old tyres, prams with wheels missing, the lot.

This was our favourite area when we had a break from the football.

Indeed, such affection did this clump of trees hold for us that years later one of my best schoolboy pals from our Crosslee days together, Malcolm Roberts—at that time one of Britain's top singing stars with a record 'Love Is All' at number two in the charts, recently returned from South America, where he won the Song Contest for Great Britain—came round to see me one afternoon at 30 Clough Top, and during our chat he said "Do you fancy climbing the Big Oak?" Two minutes later a world-famous singer and a fully grown professional footballer were sat atop the 'Big Oak' in the middle of the afternoon surveying their former kingdom, much to the amazement of 'The Ikey' (park keeper to non-Blackley people), who was begging us to come down and "Not to be silly".

Whit Sunday, was, to put it mildly, a bit of a drag. It was the one day in the year when you had to wear your new suit.

Parents each year bought their children Whit Sunday clothes and you would then be sent to show them off to your relatives.

You would squeak to their homes in your new shoes, stand to attention, Grandma would say "Oh! you are a smart boy" and slip you a half-crown into your top pocket. It could be a lucrative day but Oh! what a drag. "No kicking a ball in those new shoes," my Mother would warn me as I left the house to go on my rounds.

I met up with Malc Roberts this particular Whit Sunday. I'd never seen him looking so smart. He was resplendent in new suit, new shirt, tie, everything; his Mam had really done him proud.

There was nothing to do in Blackley on Whit Sunday so we decided to hop on the bus to town. We quickly realised that there was nothing to do anywhere on Whit Sunday as we wandered around Manchester like Wyatt Earp and his partner walking through a ghost town. Then it started to rain and we didn't want to get wet so we dived into the only place that was open, The Manchester Art Gallery.

The only thing I knew about painting was when I'd helped

my Dad paint the kitchen wall, but at least we kept our new clothes dry and that was the main thing.

"What a nice thing to see young people taking an interest in art," a sophisticated voice whispered in our ears. We both looked round to see a very nice lady obviously so sincere in her comments that we didn't have the heart to disappoint her.

"Yes, we pop down whenever we can between studies," I replied in my poshest accent, thinking this would satisfy her, but her comments became more profound.

"This is a Constable collection as you probably know," she went on. "Yes, I love his work," said I knowingly, "I think he should pack the Police Force in and paint full time, don't you, Malcolm?" who nodded his head approvingly. We were obviously saying the correct things because shortly afterwards she wrote to both our headmasters saying that we were a credit to our schools and used to send us miniature 'Constable' postcards until the day she died.

We never had the heart to tell her the truth.

However, it had brightened up a bit by now so we were off home. As we were walking for our bus we did at last see another human being in Manchester that day, although to us Mancunians at the time he was regarded as superhuman. It was Brian Statham, the famous Lancashire and England fast bowler, the terror of Australian batsmen, who was walking towards us on Mosley Street . It was too good a chance to miss, we literally bowled him over in our rush to obtain his autograph and we sat excitedly on the back seat of the 112 bus to 'The Ben Brierley' discussing the day and the excitement of getting Brian's autograph.

'The Ben Brierley' is a well-known Moston pub which doubled as a bus terminus on the opposite side of Boggart Hole Clough to where we both lived, so we had to walk through the park to get home because the buses were not running any further that day.

This was to prove fatal because it meant we had to pass by our favourite haunt 'The Hollows'.

It was just how we had left it the previous day, all our favourite trees were there looking very inviting, but we managed to resist the urge to climb them. Our thick 'Tarzan' rope was hanging from our tree. When it was pulled up to the top of the 'Hollow' we could swing across the abyss and back again. High above the muddy, rust-filled, stinking, slimy stream we would soar just like Johnny Weissmuller, but no not today, not in our best Whit-week clothes.

The rope swung to and fro tantalizingly.

"I'll just have one go," I said and grabbed the rope, ran it back up the hill until it was taut. "AAAAAH!!" I shouted as I flew through the air and back, to land nimbly on my feet, back where I started from.

Malc couldn't resist it either, and with great care he put his piece of paper, with the Brian Statham autograph on it, gently between his teeth; not his lips because he didn't want the paper to get wet or the ink would run. Then he was ready and he set off. High in the air he flew; he was at the peak of his flight when the unbelievable happened—the branch simply snapped and from about 20ft. in the air Malcolm splashed down into the stagnant morass below him. He plunged like a bird with its wings clipped. He didn't make a splash, more of a splodge, as he sank from sight, just his head visible.

An Olympic judge would probably have awarded about 7-8 for technical merit. I awarded it 10 out of 10 as my knees buckled with uncontrollable laughter at the sight before me; never have I laughed so much before or since than I did that day. Who needs enemies with a friend like me?

Malc lay flat on his back, all his best Whit-week clothes ruined, with only his head just above the surface. Whilst I tried to regain my composure on top of the hill he shouted to me through clenched teeth that still gripped the precious piece of paper "It's all right, don't worry, I managed to keep the autograph dry!"

I'm sure Mrs Roberts was pleased to hear that.

six

THE DEAN AND I

I was now beginning to relish the competitive side of football. Much better than simply training or practising on my own. Saturday was nicely taken care of, school game on a Saturday morning—one of the school teams always had a fixture—City or United Saturday afternoon.

Sunday mornings I now went down into 'The Clough' to pit my wits and shooting ability against Joe Dean. Joe was the current local hero. Manchester Boys goalkeeper, England Schoolboys goalkeeper, he had taken over the title of 'Blackley Boy Makes Good' from Wilf McGuinness who had gone through the stages of schoolboy football to captain England and eventually play for Manchester United.

I saw Wilf play most of his games for Manchester Boys. My next-door neighbours, Auntie Alice and Uncle Ernie, took me to the big schoolboy games at Maine Road to cheer him on and he really was an outstanding player.

Now Joe was heading the same way and every Sunday morning he would be like an old-time prize fighter taking on all-comers, inviting them to try their luck in scoring past him.

He was like a colossus, and looked superbly fit, a giant of a youth with huge safe hands. I used to give my shots everything I had, really concentrating and connecting with some beauties, but just when I thought that I had beaten him an enormous hand would reach out and scoop the ball up with consummate ease, or if he was in a little difficulty four fingers like a plate of sausages would tip my effort round the post.

As the weeks went by my frustrations grew more and more in my attempts to beat him. I would be up early on Sundays with my boots on waiting for him to arrive about nine-thirty; by twelve-thirty I was on my way back home dejectedly trudging back for my dinner, having failed again. Three hours of non-stop shooting, my legs felt as though I was wearing concrete boots and I still hadn't managed to put one past him.

This went on for twelve months until he signed for Bolton Wanderers and NOT ONCE did I manage to score against him.

In later years I played against him when he kept goal for Bolton Wanderers and never scored, and also when he played for Carlisle United and also never scored.

Since we have both retired I have played against him in charity matches many times and still haven't scored. I must beat him at least once before we go to the great Wembley in the sky.

There was, however, a bit of a void on Sunday afternoons. I could always just go down to the hockey pitch to train, but really I now wanted games, but there were none on a Sunday afternoon.

One particular Sunday we reached an all-time low. I was with my bosom pal Mike Roddy patrolling the streets looking for a game. We were really struggling because disaster had struck, somebody had pinched our ball. Imagine, Sunday afternoon and no ball, we were like a couple of stray tom cats in search of scraps as we covered Blackley in search of a game. Eventually we saw a particularly obnoxious kid sat in his bedroom window. This lad was not one of our gang, we disliked him intensely, but one thing in his favour was that he always had all the gear.

In the summer he would not only have wickets but bails as well, a corky with a seam and proper wicket-keeping gloves. Unbelievable, we thought his Dad was a bank robber! We had a piece of wood and a tenniser (tennis ball) with a lamp post for wickets and the first crack in the pavement was the crease. When we went to the baths we didn't have trunks, we had a

'V' neck Fair Isle pullover. We'd slip our legs through the arm-holes, hold it up with a snake belt, and dive in. When we hit the water it would hold in the wool, weigh us down, and then would finish down round our ankles exposing ourselves to the world. We never went in for mixed bathing! But he had flippers, snorkel and goggles.

Our hopes for a game rose when we spied him this day. It was a bit of a sacrifice to allow him to play with us, but we quickly weighed things up and felt it was worth putting up with him. It was the least we could do.

"Dennis," I shouted up to him, feeling like the lead actor in the balcony scene from 'Romeo and Juliet'.

"Are you coming out to play and bring your ball?" Dennis amazed by his sudden rise in the popularity stakes shouted down enthusiastically, "Yes, I'm coming out to play, but my ball's burst". "See you Dennis," came the reply as Mike and I wended our weary way. When you are desperate you will try anything!

We were now suffering from severe withdrawal symptoms and in a flash of genius I came up with the answer to fill in our Sunday afternoons. We will form a team of our own. If we have our own team we will never be short of a game, I reasoned. It was the ideal solution and I, of course, would assume the role of player/manager, penalty taker, corner-kick taker, taker of the throw-ins, free kicks and anything else that was going. How could we go wrong?

So I became a manager for the first time at the age of twelve. I soon recruited the best players in Blackley and challenged anybody foolish enough to pass through the district.

We had a good team, with relatively few selection problems. It was simple, my best mates played in which ever of the other ten positions they fancied (the number 9 shirt was reserved exclusively for me) and those further down my social roster had what was left. I don't know why the Football League Man-agers make such a big fuss of the job!

Of course, at times disciplinary action had to be taken. There was a time when one lad said he would get me a Blackpool programme because he was going to stay at his Grandma's who lived at the seaside. He forgot, so was promptly axed from the team for the next match.

You have got to be firm with these players!

Especially after a serious indiscretion such as this.

Did Ron Greenwood really start this way?

seven

WHITE HART–BREAK LANE

As a result of all my activity out of school my football was improving enormously, but unfortunately the same cannot be said about my school work.

When the time came to streamline my subjects it was a difficult decision for me because I was poor at them all. I decided to take commerce, my reasoning being that when I had completed my career as a star footballer a knowledge of commerce, however scant, would stand me in good stead when I took the customary newsagent's shop. It was all figured out, but Mr Castley, our commerce teacher, was not that confident. During our lessons my mind would wander to the next game and try as I may I just could not seem to concentrate on my school work.

I found it particularly hard this Wednesday afternoon in 1957 when City had a vital replay and were kicking off at two-fifteen. They had drawn at Newcastle on the Saturday and today was replay day; what I would have given to have been there.

I toyed with the idea of 'becoming ill' on the big day, but this idea was quickly removed from my mind when the teacher said to me the day before ''Even if you are feeling half dead, I advise you to come in tomorrow because yours is the first face I shall be looking for''. Ah! the price of fame!

So I had to content myself with a place at my desk, calculating the score by the loudness of the roars. What a game it was, my ears were like decibel meters as I followed the game kick by kick. A few near misses, one or two "Ooo's" and an odd "Aah!" then four o'clock came—home time. The game had been over five minutes and as I came out of school I would just catch the first of the supporters on their way home. They, I was sure, would disprove all my calculations that City had lost 4-5; what a ridiculous score, who could beat City 4-5 at home ... in the cup as well, out of the question, I had obviously read the roars wrongly.

I raced down Denmark Road and shouted to the first man I saw decked out in sky blue and white "What was the score mate?"

"They lost five-four," came the reply that stopped me in my tracks. My calculations were correct, if only I was as good at maths!

"They brought in a lad at centre forward called Alex Tait. He was brilliant, never heard of him before, red hair just like you."

"Never heard of him before," and he puts us out of the cup. No Wembley for me this year. It's the one time in my life I wanted to be proved wrong.

Soon Manchester Boys trials came round and the school sent five of us in for the trials. It was a tremendous honour to play for Manchester Boys, if you made the team you were under constant scrutiny by the top clubs and indeed a host of famous players had reached the top after playing for Manchester Boys. Finally from the thousands of boys a squad of eighteen was announced including two from our school, my mate Bob Smith and myself.

Football had brought Bob and I together. He had missed the whole of the first year's schooling and also the all-important trials for the school team, so he had been a late starter.

Indeed, if it had not been for me he may have been a nonstarter. Because of all the time he had off school with illness the teachers didn't know if he was any good or not, but being a fellow North Manchester lad I had seen him perform in the

Clough and was able to put in a good word with the teacher. Now he was making up for lost time.

We were both selected for all the opening fixtures, him at right back and me in front of him at right half, two gingernuts together although he insists to this day that his is auburn ..... both strands.

The team remained the same as we won all our games.

My eyes were set firmly on 'The Big One' in one week's time, away to London Boys, when I would achieve another of my ambitions and play on a football league ground for the first time.

The game was to be played at White Hart Lane, the home of Tottenham Hotspur, under floodlights as well, it would be a wonderful experience. But first we had to dispose of St. Helen's Boys on Saturday, before leaving for London on Tuesday to stay overnight in London, play the game at night and return home the next day. Just like a proper footballer, I'd better get used to this if this is going to be my life for the next fifteen years!

Secretly I had not been really happy with my form; the selectors seemed pleased enough, I was picked for all the games, we won them all handsomely with me in the side, so these thoughts reassured me and I kept pushing my fears to the back of my mind.

The problem was that something I had wanted badly all my life was now within my grasp. A final push and I would be there, I would be offered a job on the groundstaff of some club, hopefully City, all I had to do was play well. I was a good player, I knew that, I was as good, if not better than most of the other players in the team, with an excellent, almost un-paralleled playing record behind me to back me up ..... but I was becoming too anxious, I couldn't relax when the day of the game came round. My old carefree, confident style wasn't really there. I was trying too hard to impress the all-seeing eyes of the 'scouts' who were watching. I was my own, most diffi-cult opponent and whilst I played tensely and averagely, other players with less skill were playing with gay abandon and playing well ..... but we were winning and that was the main thing, and when I got a couple more games under my belt maybe I would relax a bit and enjoy myself.

Roll on White Hart Lane!

Before boarding the coach for the trip to St. Helen's I had gone to Littlewoods with my Mother to choose my first holdall. "You'll have to have one for all those overnight stays you will be having from now on," she said, and I chose a smashing blue one—no other colour would do! She took it home for me to iron and pack my gear for London whilst I went to fight the foe at St. Helen's.

The coach arrived at the school in St. Helen's, ironically in a street called Frederick Street, and I tried to convince myself that this was a good omen as I tried to do battle with my nerves again and keep them under control.

I thought I was succeeding and was appearing outwardly calm, laughing and singing all the 'Everley Brothers' hits with the boys when 'whoosh'; I thought somebody had tipped a bowl of tomato soup over me as my lap filled up with blood. It cascaded from my nose like Niagara Falls, completely ruining my clothes.

"Don't tell Whetton," I whispered to Bob, who had by this time dived out from the seat next to me to avoid any splashes ruining his brand new suit, a delicate little number from 'Damien's Tailors of Distinction' on Moston Lane. A few red dots would have completed his ensemble. Mr Whetton was the team Manager and was the most miserable man I had ever met until then. Or since then, come to think of it. I'm sure if he ever smiled his face would crack. My lace came undone during one game, I managed to tie it just in time to score the winning goal for Manchester Boys. I was met by a volley of abuse as I got back to the dressing-room for not being able to tie my boots properly. The goal never got a mention.

He was now sat at the front of the coach with his number two, Cain. What a pair, and I was sure if he heard of my predicament I would have been out of the team.

As the coach arrived in Frederick Street, I quickly wrapped

my gaberdine around me to cover up the mess and hurried quickly into the dressing-room.

What with my nerves and my nose I was in a fine mess. Just let me get through the game.

I was fast losing sight of the most important thing, that football is a game to enjoy. Take it seriously by all means, but above all enjoy it.

In future years as I became a coach myself and handled hundreds of young kids on trial, I would always try to relax them early on, tell them they were under no pressure. "Don't try to impress me," I would say, "Just do your best and enjoy yourself."

I certainly wasn't enjoying myself this day, I was just about getting through the game, a little bit here, a little bit there. Bob behind me was having a storming game, constantly surging forward on overlaps, years before they were even invented, and I was doing a useful little job covering the gaps he left. He was certainly making up for lost time!

At the final whistle we had won 4-0 and I was pleased that the game was out of the way. I'll make London Boys suffer on Wednesday instead.

We were all in high spirits as the coach chugged its way back to Manchester down the East Lancs Road. For the entire journey Whetton and Cain had been huddled together on the front seat like a couple of secret agents. Finally, he silenced us between choruses of 'Bird-dog' and 'Singing The Blues', as he came down the aisle of the bus with a crumpled scrap of paper in his hand, his drooping moustache twitching.

"This is the team for the game against London on Wednesday," and he began to trot out the familiar names; Brian Greenhalgh in goal, Joe Clayton right back. I don't believe it, Bob's been dropped, I thought he had a great game. I looked at him quickly in the seat next to me; he looked grim. Left back Peter Jackson, right half Bob Smith; relief on Bob's face, I must be left half. I'd played there before, poor old Mike Rabbitt is going to be out of the side as I am switched to left half. Rabbitt and Eyre—what a pair of wing halves we made, a couple of 'Bunnies,' we didn't get measles, we got myxamotosis!

Centre half Alan Atherton, he went on, left half Mike Rabbitt. My heart sank to my boots. O-U-T. What a blow. In the next few seconds I managed to pull myself together sufficiently enough to convince everybody that I had taken it well.

I'd never been to London anyway, I consoled myself, so it will be a nice couple of days' holiday and maybe somebody will fall ill! "The following players are travelling reserves." Again my name was missing; I was for the first time in my life completely shattered, it was a feeling I was to get to know many times in the future.

How they could leave me out of the squad when I had played in every game and take the five reserves, none of whom had even yet kicked a ball for the team, was just too much for me to comprehend.

I got off the coach in Piccadilly, not a word was said to me by Whetton or Cain. I walked down Market Street like a zombie, nipped into the first back alley, Cromford Court, and was physically sick down the nearest grid.

The journey home on the 26 bus seemed to take a lifetime.

The door of number 30 was opened by my Dad, I brushed aside his usual first question "How did you get on?" and collapsed on to the settee and cried for an hour. I never played for Manchester Boys again.

Being the true sportsman that I am, I hoped that they would get hammered 5-0 and that Whetton would be crawling round to our house admitting a severe error of judgement and would I please, please, play for Manchester Boys in all their remaining fixtures.

I was sitting on the stairs waiting to catch the 'Daily Express' before it hit the floor, the morning after the game, to find out the score.

There was a good picture of Ernie Ackerley scoring the fifth in a "superb 5-0 win for Manchester Boys" as the headline screamed.

What a choker! At least I GOT THE SCORE RIGHT.

I was glad for my mates but sad inside. Players throughout

the world over will know the mixed emotion; it's only a natural one ..... I hope.

However, I was finished before I'd even started. Bob, who took my place, went on to play for Lancashire Boys and England Boys, at Wembley, God bless him. I don't know how but he's still my oldest friend to this day!

He certainly made up for lost time! He was kind enough to bring me back the Programme, with my name in the number 4 position, I still have it to this day. I would have been playing against Martin Peters; what a narrow escape for him!

My main problem now was how could I get taken on by a league club when I'm not being watched regularly for Manchester Boys.

It was back to 'The Clough' for me ..... back to the hockey pitch ..... back to the drawing board.

eight

"SENT FOR TRIAL"

Blackley lads have always been blessed with a bit of spirit. Les Dawson, who lived behind the shops near me, struggled for years as a small-time comedian and piano player in working men's clubs all over the North of England and in dives and places of ill repute in Paris, but his Blackley spirit kept him plugging away until he finally hit the jackpot.

The same with Bernard Manning—he has not always been 'big'! He knows the meaning of the word graft. Singing all night for the big bands and helping to run the family green-grocery business by day.

My old hero Wilf McGuinness , after scaling the heights for Manchester United and gaining a full England Cap plunged in-to the depths, with a broken leg of such severity that it finally finished his soccer career as a player.

But not before he had made superhuman efforts to make a comeback; he typified the Blackley spirit.

Now it was my chance to prove that I was up there with the best of them in this department, if nothing else.

I'd done it before, even though I knew nothing about it at the time, when the medics thought I was 'a goner' as a baby after I had contracted double pneumonia and pleurisy, but even then I was a true Blackley Baby by pulling through, with much nursing from anxious parents. But I was a big boy now, and after the initial shock had worn off and I started eating again,

I threw myself into my training even harder than before.

As well as my open air, hockey pitch ball work, I devised a set of exercises and a little circuit to do every evening in the kitchen when I got home from school.

This would entail press-ups, trunk curls on the kitchen floor and step ups on the kitchen chair, all performed whilst my Mother was preparing the tea. During this time she also developed into being pretty nifty on her feet, as she learned to avoid my prostrate grunting body with amazing dexterity.

At the end of my fifteen-minutes circuit I would be covered in sweat. I didn't realise this was due to the steam from the pressure cooker until we had a salad for tea one night and I wasn't sweating when I'd finished my circuit.

I kept this routine going all through the season right through to Cup Final Day.

Cup Final Day was and still is one of the main events of the 'Fred Eyre Social Calendar'. I love everything about Cup Final Day.

The weather is invariably beautiful, all the players, no matter how hard a season they have had, always look in peak condition. New kit especially for the occasion, fresh and clean.

The Ground filled to capacity, the turf lush and green, the stripes seemingly cut with slide rule precision and the community singing. Fantastic. I'm not a hymn-singing person, but the present-day practice of singing rude songs while the band plays 'Abide With Me' really sickens me.

It used to typify the spirit of the game, ten minutes before the kick off both sets of supporters singing this great song in unison—together, then as soon as the whistle blows cheer your own team on. Alas, not now it seems.

Every Cup Final Day Uncle Gus would come in from next door. For as long as I can remember Uncle Gus had been of bad health, I can't ever remember him working, he was stuck indoors all days wheezing and coughing and we all knew he would die shortly.

In fact one night we thought he had died. It was lashing down with rain, it always is with emergencies, when one of his daughters rushed to our house to say if he didn't have a tablet within 30 minutes he would die, and they hadn't any tablets.

At that time we were the only family in Clough Top Road with a car to make the necessary journey to the all night Boots Chemist in town so my Dad grabbed his coat and dashed out in the monsoon to the little car parked at the kerb, trying to put his coat on as he ran.

One arm in, a quick swing round the shoulders and clink, the keys flew out of his pocket and slithered along the gutter. Before they even reached the grid I could see from the doorway what was going to happen, we stood tranfixed as slither slither ..... plop right down the drain they went.

My poor Dad was already blaming himself for Uncle Gus's death. Visions of the funeral flashed before our eyes, then he was down on his face in the gutter in a flash trying to get his hand through the narrow iron slats. No chance—there was only me for it. I could get my whole arm in, right up to my shoulder, but as I fingered amongst the slime, torrential rain beating down on my back, my right ear ploughing a furrow through the mud, I couldn't get the keys. Eventually after much rooting about and scooping, I came up with the treasure and Uncle Gus was now enjoying another Cup Final.

He had four daughters, who obviously knew nothing about football, so he would come in, we would get our shandies ready, a quarter of chocolate caramels, draw the curtains and never move from the TV set until the last player had disappeared down the tunnel from his lap of honour. We must have looked a strange pair, but it was great.

I had been to Wembley once, the year before; unfortunately it wasn't City. I had had the pleasure of that, on TV, for two successive years, when first of all they lost to Newcastle. When Bobby Johnstone dived to head the equaliser I dived along with him off the settee. That year was a defeat but the next year, as skipper Roy Paul had promised us all, we were back to win it, little Joe Hayes putting us in front after just a couple of minutes when Don Revie back heeled it to him, what joy.

But this time I was going to see United; it was a bit below the belt I must admit, but a trip to Wembley doesn't come up every day.

We had been invited for tea by our friends the Coldricks. Uncle Stan's Dad worked on the turnstile at Old Trafford and used to give me a bit of stick about City.

When I got there I was asked if I would like 'a butty' and a glass of milk. Never one to refuse food, I didn't give the sandwich a second look as I took a huge mouthful; the filling tasted a bit cardboardy and carefully peeling apart the two pieces of bread all was revealed ..... a Cup Final Ticket. I preferred that to boiled ham that's for sure, what a lovely surprise, I must make sure he has one of the best seats when I lead City out at Wembley!

City did get to Wembley again in the next decade, but I had been and gone by then.

I was back with my shandy and caramels watching, as Neil Young my pal and holiday partner—we had a super week together in Blackpool one year—smashed in the only goal past Peter Shilton to beat Leicester City. If it couldn't be me then I was glad it was him.

However, this Cup Final day Nottingham Forest had just beaten Luton and the spectacle of the day had made me eager for a game so I rounded up Mike Roddy and it was down to the hockey pitch as usual.

The game was in full flow. I remember I was feeling particularly perky when my Dad appeared from the bushes; this was very strange, he never came down the 'The Clough', it must be something very important. "You had better get back up to the house, there's somebody from City to see you."

The words I had waited fifteen years to hear—it was music to my ears, I grabbed my coat and dashed back home.

Enjoying a cup of coffee with my Mother was the figure of Harry Godwin, a check overcoat, smart shirt and tie, a fine representative of the club.

Harry was a super person, ideal for the job of scout for a club like City and to make things even better, a Blackley man

He has been responsible for signing nearly all City's young stars over the years.

Peter Barnes, Gary Owen, Mike Doyle, Neil Young, Dave Wagstaffe, Paul Power, Glyn Pardoe, Alan Oakes and a host of others who went on to become top names in the game.

Surely with a record like that he can be forgiven for making one mistake, because now he was wanting to sign me ..... or was he?

While I was wondering where my best pen was, I wanted to to sign in my best writing, Harry was quietly pouring a little cold water on my enthusiasm.

The majority of my former team mates had now been offered groundstaff contracts with the big clubs. Bob Smith, Dave Latham and Ernie Ackerley had signed for United, Ken Fletcher and Neil Young for City and so on, "But due to the fact that you weren't in the Manchester Boys team for such a long spell," Harry went on, "the best we can offer you is a trial".

"A trial ..... Bloody Hell," I thought, "I'm going to have to prove myself all over again," and I knew inwardly I was not at my best when I was subjected to that sort of pressure.

I was able to perform much better when I was at ease with the world. But I had two choices, "take it or leave it", so I took it, shook Harry's hand at the door and watched him walk briskly up Clough Top until his muscular frame disappeared round the corner at the top.

As I turned back into the house I was met by huge smiles and grins of well done by my Mam and Dad. Only for me to ungratefully return them with a grim, tight-lipped, "Flippin' Trial".

The day of reckoning came when I had to report at 6 pm to Shawe View Field, Chassen Road, Urmston, for my trial on August 4th 1959. It was a glorious day, the sun shone incessantly the whole day long. We were in the middle of our Summer Holidays, everybody was outdoors breathing in the glorious fresh air ..... except me, I stayed in bed the whole day reading and conserving all my energy, quite wrongly reasoning that I would unleash it all on the other unsuspecting trialists that evening.

Chassen Road was two bus rides and a train journey away but I seemed to be there in no time and I walked in with my gear to be met by the first of a breed of men who were to play an important part in my soccer life in the future .....the coach. His name was Jim Meadows and he was the first in a line of 82 coaches whose job it was at one stage or another to shape my career. That together with my 29 Managers makes a hell of a lot of bosses.

nine

COACHES

Not including the Manager Les McDowell, and Assistant Manager George Poyser, there were seven coaches at Manchester City when I arrived. More than Finglands, the coach firm who took us to away games had!

Since my introduction to coaches I've come across some classic cases. One said to me before one game "I want you to do a Pacific job for me today," I don't think I endeared myself to him by replying "Well you'll have to give me oceans of room then".

Another said to me knowingly out of the corner of his mouth before a game at Grimsby,"I've been out and it's very windy tonight, so I suggest you keep your high balls low". Others have said things with the best of intentions but still can't get it right. Our coach at Bradford said "Fred, I want you to play today like you've never played before ..... I want you to play well"; that really spurred me on.

Coaches are usually at their best at half-time when things are not quite going to plan.

"Too many of our square balls are going through the middle" one screamed at us at Scunthorpe during the half-time break.

In one of my teams we had a player alongside me in the back four who had a bad stammer. I used to make a few bob off him playing snap with him for money! For some inexplicable reason the boss put him in charge of our offside trap, before he could shout oo--uut however we would be a goal down.

In the end he asked the Boss to ''relieve him of the re-responsibility''.

I used to take the mickey out of him a bit about his stammer, so much so that one day he turned on me and said ''I'm ssorry I ever told you I ha had a blo--bloody stammer!''.

I couldn't believe it when in later years he became a manager. If ever there was anybody less suited to be a Manager it was him, I could believe it even less when he made me his first signing.

''If y--you f--fancy signing g--give m--me a r--ring at home, if nobody answers that w--will be m-mee'' he said.

I think I signed out of curiosity and he didn't let me down. Before the game he said ''We are not playing 4-3-3 today, I'm scrapping it and we are playing a new system.

''We'll have 4 at the back the same as before, 3 up front the same as before, but only **two** in midfield and you, Fred, I want you to play in between the two!''

It sounded very much like 4-3-3 to me but after all he is the coach!

Another superb example of coaching and attention to detail was the day we kicked off at 6.15 pm during the electricity crisis to save the expense of the floodlights. At seven o'clock we were all sat in the dressing-room at half time, boots caked with mud, mud stained shirts and shorts, sweat stained faces, ball marks in the centre of foreheads where we had occasionally headed one correctly, steaming cups of tea in ten pairs of grubby, muddy hands (I was the odd one out, I don't drink tea) a player on the treatment table receiving treatment for a gashed knee and we were all on the receiving end of a severe bollocking from our coach because we were losing 0-1 at home.

The door opened, stopping our coach in full flight, and the senior coach came in and took over the conversation.

''All the best today lads, go at them straight from the kick off contain them a bit in the first half and then our stamina will tell in the second.''

I looked round at the mud-stained filthy looking players in the dressing room, furrowed a caked muddy brow and enquired quietly to our chief coach did he think we always went out to start a match dressed like this and we didn't usually sweat so much whilst simply drinking tea!

He sheepishly had to admit he thought it was a seven o'clock kick off.

He went one better later in the season when we played a cup tie against much stronger opposition than us away from home.

His plan was "to contain them right from the kick off". We would pull every man back, man for man mark, play a sweeper behind the sweeper and employ every defensive tactic in the book to ensure a nil-nil draw and a replay. Our instructions were not to push up beyond the half-way line but to sit in our own half and defend and boot every ball and human being that came near.

With these instructions firmly into our heads we left the dressing-room; we lost the toss and kicked off.

Straight from the kick off the ball was knocked out to our right winger, who beat two men on the flank, got to the bye line, put over a picture cross and much to our delight it was headed gleefully into the net by our number 10.

Our jubilations were short-lived, however, because the coach was screaming from the dug-out.

"Can't you do anything I tell you, you've ruined the entire plan, you're on your own now for the next 88 minutes, don't look to me for any help."

We eventually lost 1-2. He said at the end "What do you expect if you don't follow my instructions"!

Before another game, he boosted my confidence by telling me that the winger I was marking that day was "absolute rubbish". "He can't cross a ball', he informed me. "I've seen him five times this season and he looks good as he flies past his opposing full-back, but then instead of hitting a good centre into the penalty box, he crosses them straight into the net. Hopeless!"

But all those were in the future, first of all I had Jim. Jim

Meadows came to City as a right winger from Southport, was successfully converted to full-back and was such a success that he gained an England Cap.

Unfortunately he sustained a serious knee injury in the 1955 Cup Final defeat by Newcastle United (which cost City the Cup) and his playing career came to an abrupt end.

Now he was in charge of the young kids and I took an immediate liking to him, but like most of the other lads I was a bit frightened of him. He was always very good to me but I made sure I never stepped out of line.

My fears in this direction were confirmed when later in the season Dave Shawcross, a highly talented wing half whose career ironically went the same way as Jim's, England Under 23 Cap, then a serious knee injury at Molineux after colliding with Wolves keeper Malcolm Finlayson, ruined his career, had the nerve to give Jim a bit of back-chat which wasn't exactly to Jim's liking.

'Shawcy' was in the bath at the time, wallowing like a contented hippo, lathering himself with soap when Jim appeared in the doorway after hearing his remark.

'Shawcy' took one look at Jim's face, leapt from the bath, ran through the dressing-room, down the players' tunnel completely naked, soap suds streaming from his body, across the pitch with Jim racing in pursuit, his bad leg temporarily forgotten, brandishing his fist like a side of ham.

'Shawcy's' fitness was the key factor together with his fear. It gave him a bit of extra impetus as he ran the length of the field, past startled groundstaff men who were casually forking the pitch. Over the wall, up the terraces then he clambered up the rickety steps into the sanctuary of the scoreboard and locked himself in.

Jim finally arrived on the scene and positioned himself at the foot of the ladder to wait until the shivering, naked, 'Shawcy' decided to give himself up.

It was a funny sight to see Dave's head poking through the squares where usually the half-time scores were displayed, trying to figure a way out.

Jim 1. 'Shawcy' 0!

But this evening back at Urmston I was to be spoken to by a coach for the first time in my life, and I was already convinced that I would go home a better player.

We sat round Jim crosslegged in a circle on the floor. He looked like an Adonis standing over us in his blue tracksuit and his first words will live with me for ever.

"You can all sit closer to me than this, I've not got shit on my shoes."

Not a bad start! Things can only improve after that.

Things did improve and I settled down well. I always found Jim a hard taskmaster but he was always fair with me, which was to be a rarity with coaches and Managers, as I was to find out over the years.

There were over 1,000 trialists passing through the dressing-rooms of Chassen Road in the next six weeks of which two were signed as amateurs. One of them left two weeks after he signed, so that left just me ..... one in 1,000, and it was a never to be forgotten day when I signed, leaning on the window ledge of Harry Godwin's house on Victoria Avenue ..... in Blackley it had to be! Still not a full groundstaff contract but a start. Maybe if I impressed in the games I would get a contract.

I felt confident of improving under the whip of Jim and the gentle touch of Dick Niellson, but never got the chance.

A reshuffle of the ranks at the club found Jim promoted to first team coach in place of Laurie Barnett, who moved over to be physio.

Laurie had been at the club a lifetime. He was a former full-back who was now getting on in years, was very hard of hearing and if he didn't want to be bothered with anything he simply used to switch off his hearing aid.

He had seen it all and his lack of enthusiasm and dour exterior didn't really endear him to the rest of the players. I myself received one single piece of advice from Laurie during the entire time I was at the club, which was a few years and I saw him every morning and almost every afternoon. "Get to the pitch of the ball," that was it.

I thought he meant the pitch we were playing on.

Fred Tilson, the reserve team trainer, was even worse; he sat all day in his little room picking horses and sleeping. I used to go back for extra training in the afternoons and had a hard job waking Fred about two o'clock for him to open the gym for me. The rattle of his keys was drowned by his moaning about me disturbing him.

Fred was a legend at Manchester City. He had scored two goals in the 1934 Cup Final and that seemed to ensure him a job for life.

I also received one single piece of advice from Fred in all my time at the club.

"You should have your bleedin' tonsils out," he informed me in his thick Barnsley accent, as I complained one day of a sore throat.

Jim McLelland, an elderly Scottish gentleman, was the 'A' team coach at the time. He was assisted by a part-timer, Joe Mycock, who used to smoke a pipe like 'Popeye' and tell us jokes in the dressing-room before we took the field.

Jim also gave me one pearl of wisdom when he got all of us groundstaff lads together and informed us that football was "like a wortch", said in a gentle, lilting, Scottish accent; "if one part isn't working it falls out of gear".

We all nodded appreciatively, none of us could follow the reasoning at all, but the phrase "like a wortch" became part of our vocabulary to describe absolutely anything.

"How's your ankle?"

"Well it's like a wortch," we would reply.

Jim was a kind person, but not really strong enough to cope with the lads.

The two other part-timers, Dick and Walt, I liked very much. I liked their approach to young boys, kind and warm, fairly firm but not enough to dampen either your spirit or your enthusiasm.

The fact that Dick is still doing the job to this day is a testimony to the quality of the man.

Finally there was Johnny, Johnny Hart. I desperately wanted

to like Johnny, and finally, 20 years on, I do, as I've got older and so has he, because I now understand him. But he made it terribly difficult for me to warm to him in the early days.

Secretly I had always admired him as a player and when he was in a good mood I appreciated his dry sense of humour, but I never knew where I was with him from one day to the next.

One day joke after joke tripped off his tongue, the next he would totally ignore me all day long.

I simply couldn't read his moods at all.

John hated to lose at anything, not a bad trait to possess. One day Jim Meadows and himself challenged Neil Young and I to a game of doubles at table tennis for sixpence per man. John always won; snooker, billiards, table tennis, you name it, John was always the winner.

But this day Neil and I were going quite well, and the word spread like wildfire around the club that Jim and John were in danger of losing a tanner each. The mere thought was inconceivable and soon the table tennis room was filled to capacity as the whole club cheered every point Neil and I won and hissed and booed every time Jim or John scored a lucky point.

A huge roar went up as Neil smashed in the WINNING backhand and everybody waited to witness the momentous occasion when Jim and John would actually hand over the money.

Jim laughed and tossed Neil a tanner, John scowled at me, without a word, bent down and slid the coin firmly along the floor until it came to rest right in the middle of the floor underneath the table tennis table.

"If you want it you'll have to crawl on your hands and knees to get it," he said over his shoulder as he left the scene.

The room, full of cheers a minute earlier, was now in total silence, all eyes were upon me. I looked at it shining there under the table and decided to leave it there. John certainly knew how to make you suffer.

So they were my coaches together with the Manager Les McDowell, who was always conspicuous by his absence. He made Howard Hughes seem like Bruce Forsyth by comparison, and we didn't see much more of his assistant 'Genial' George Poyser, who smoked his pipe so much it had worn all his teeth away.

George it seemed used to spend most of his time playing snooker and eating egg butties. Actually I also received my customary single piece of advice from him whilst I was recovering from a pulled muscle, "Play wi'it while you're watching TV at home", he advised me.

I presume he meant my leg!

It has to be said that a lot of players made the grade during this period, but I feel they made it in spite of the system, not because of it.

There were others who needed a bit of help along the way, a bit of guidance as we took the wrong track, and if we had received it at the correct time, would have done much better. Maybe still wouldn't have reached the top but would have done much better.

When I began coaching, I always remembered my tutors at City when I was dealing with players and it used to give my confidence in my own ability a tremendous boost.

ten

A MARS A DAY HELPS YOU WORK, REST AND PLAY

I felt my game improving playing against quality opposition every week. I had played in every game and was now quite used to the surroundings at 'Hatters Park', the little ground behind a pub in Denton where we played, but still there was no mention of a proper contract.

This was particularly frustrating because by now school work was really beginning to get me down.

I had finished a feast of a tea this horrible wet evening in mid-October, slumped in a chair to watch Eammon Andrews make a fool of himself in 'Crackerjack' followed by a quick glance at the evening paper. In very minute type at the foot of the sports page read "Tonight's Fixture Maine Road. Representative Match, Manchester v Liverpool, all the North's top young players will be on view".

I glanced out of the window; it was pitch black, the rain was lashing against the windows, and any faint notions that I had about going to watch were quickly dispersed as the thought of the exact repeat journey that I had just completed, from school, to return to Maine Road in the same area was a bit too much even for a keen lad like me.

Soon it got to six-fifteen, and I was becoming bored and restless. 'Robin Hood' which had followed 'Crackerjack', failed to hold my attention even allowing for the fact that Patrica Driscoll was playing the part of Maid Marion! So I went and checked the weather again. It had stopped raining, although it was still pretty bleak. I decided to go to the match, at least it wouldn't cost me anything because I was almost skint.

I didn't pay any bus fare. Because Ducie Avenue was near Maine Road I told the inquisitive bus conductor I was going to night school as he inspected my 'Ducie Avenue Free Bus Pass'.

Now that I was a fully fledged amateur player with the club, a quick flash of the counterfoil of my signing-on paper ensured free admittance to any game at Maine Road.

So even though I was on my own it was going to be a free night out.

My signing-on slip was my most prized possession. Apart from the proof to any disbelieving kid who I was showing off to that I did actually play for City, and the bonus of its passport into the ground, it also had on the back of it the autograph of the greatest player of the day, John Charles, the great Leeds and Wales Centre Half who had been transferred to Italy for a British record fee. I found myself standing next to him at one match and I signed him for City!

Seven o'clock, the bus slowed down at Alexandra Park and I jumped off as it went round the corner, to land in a huge puddle, my school shoes as well! It was pouring down again so I nipped in a shop and bought three Mars bars and took shelter in the doorway of some unsuspecting inhabitant of Moss Side; it was absolutely lashing down.

I saw an 88 bus going in the opposite direction, back home again, and ran out to try to catch it to return home and give the match a miss because I had a walk of about a mile to get to the ground and would be like a drowned rat when I got there, but I missed the bus and dived back into the doorway and got munched into Mars bar number one.

It tasted so lovely I immediately devoured the next one and then set out for the ground feeling a little bit more able to cope with the ravages of winter.

The final Mars bar was to be for half-time, but the other two had given me such energy that I thought I would go for my hat-trick as I walked up to the steps of the players' entrance tucking into my third.

"We've been waiting for you," said the voice of George Poyser. I hadn't realised he was a clairvoyant in his spare time, because until an hour ago I didn't even know there was a game on.

I paused in mid munch to enquire what he meant.

"One lad's cried off and we knew you would come to watch." He obviously knew more about me than I knew myself. "I've no boots," I replied, two Mars bars rising in my stomach.

"We've put Colin Barlow's out for you so get down there."

Colin Barlow was the first team regular right winger, who was a real flyer. I thought if I just put them on, the boots would do the job for me.

I'd never played on a big ground before or under floodlights. A dozen pairs of hands were helping me to get stripped, one putting my socks on whilst a maroon shirt with a big white number four was being pulled over my head; the boots were a bit tight but if they were all right for Colin in the First Division they were all right for me.

Pads ..... I had no pads; 'The Manchester Evening News' was brought, folded over and torn in half. In minute type I could read "all the North's top young players will be on view". CHRIST! I thought as it was pushed down my socks.

The bell rang, off down the tunnel, team photograph as we reached the pitch, floodlights streaming down, and my Mam and Dad sat at home thinking "Fancy Fred going to Maine Road on a night like this".

A quick roll call of the names of my team-mates as we kicked in, a quick glance to the side of the goals where I always stood at the scoreboard end, then the game started ..... "Who are we playing again?"

Chris Lawler, Ian Callaghan, England Internationals of the future nothing to me that night as I gave it everything I'd got and I was elated with our 2-1 victory. I dashed home later that night, my feet still bleeding due to Colin's boots, to tell my parents about the greatest night of my life, I think Dad was a bit disappointed that he hadn't been there, but only a mind reader like George Poyser knew I would be playing.

eleven
FOREMAN OF THE GROUNDSTAFF

That game before the eyes of the bosses convinced them that I should be offered a spot on the groundstaff and so I signed for £4 per week. As with so many more occasions in the future I found out later all the other groundstaff lads were on £5 or £6, but I didn't care, the money was secondary to me.

I'd always been good with money, always a good saver, never spent anything I didn't have. "If you want something, save up for it," my Dad always said to me. "Never borrow, if you can't afford it ..... do without."

He always set me a fine example regarding money. He used to encourage me to put all my shillings into a little box with a slot in it ..... I was 21 before I realised it was the gas meter!

Now I was to earn my living as a footballer, my life's ambition. But first there was the problem of leaving school. They wouldn't let me. I didn't realise I was so valuable to them! So I had to pay the school £20 compensation in order to leave.

After me putting the name of the school on the map too!

Eventually it was all sorted out and on 7th December 1959 my life began at Maine Road.

There were no such things as Apprentice Professionals in those days, although when they came into being a couple of years later I had the distinction of being the first ever apprentice professional footballer of Manchester City Football Club.

There were five of us on the groundstaff at the time and

because I had the status 'foreman of the groundstaff' I was sent for first, signed, and then told to go and find the others for them to be converted from 'Groundstaff lads' to Apprentices'. Every other young player signed from that day was to be known as an apprentice.

Being 'foreman of the groundstaff' is just being the most senior, probably your last year before the club decides either to sign you as a full professional or to sack you.

Sometimes when lads were at the club from long distances on week's trials etc., I would be asked to look after them and take them out at night and make them feel at home.

I remember I was 'Nanny' to Dave Clements, who went on to Captain and indeed Manage Northern Ireland, picking up 40 odd caps during his career with Coventry and Everton.

Ironically I next met him some fifteen years later when he captained the famous New York Cosmos. We played them in the mighty Giant Stadium in New Jersey, and as we tossed up in the centre circle he couldn't believe his eyes as I reminded him of the time I had to look after him.

John Hurst was another of my 'Charges' when he came over from his Blackpool home for a week. John was a very quiet boy, easy to look after, and I think has remained that way in his long career as a star with Everton and Oldham Athletic.

The only time during my time as 'foreman of the groundstaff' when I had to assert my authority came the Saturday after Good Friday.

The first team had played on the Good Friday and we were to be in at 9 am the following morning to clean all the boots and get the skip ready, because they were off to play away early on Saturday.

This meant we groundstaff lads all had to leave home at eight, work till dinner time, then play our own game in the afternoon, arriving home about seven o'clock in the evening — eleven hours. A working morning, followed by a hard game, all with no food.

There was a little kitchen at Maine Road with a tiny grill and a gas ring where endless cups of coffee were supplied to the office staff, and to Fred Tilson to try to keep him awake, so I suggested to Mrs Dobell, the Maître de of the ovens that we five groundstaff lads would club together to buy a loaf and could she spare us the use of her kitchen for about ten minutes so we could make some toast so we wouldn't have to play on an empty stomach.

You would have thought we had asked for a banquet; we were buying the bread, toasting it ourselves but we couldn't reason with her. There was only one course of action to take, a trip to the office of Mr Walter Griffiths, the overlord of the whole club. I marched down to his office, my steps becoming slower and slower as I neared the end of the corridor.

I stepped where no groundstaff boy had ever stepped before—into the hallowed office of Mr Griffiths—and presented our case with a veiled threat of strike action if our demands were not met.

He accompanied me back to the waiting Mrs Dobell, told her to "use her loaf" and even to poach us an egg to go on top of our toast.

I was beginning to have views and principles of my own, but I wasn't so confident on my first day.

As I had read in countless boy's soccer magazines over the years, a groundstaff boy does all the menial tasks. Sweep the terraces, sweep and mop out the dressing-rooms each day, clean the baths and toilets each day and clean the boots.

Unlike most of the lads I quite enjoyed doing the boots—was this one really the one Joe Hayes scored with at Wembley?

Bert Trautmann's size tens were a formidable task, but I always did them extra well because he was my favourite. I was always in awe of Bert, our world famous blond German Goalkeeper. I had marvelled at his performances between the posts for so many years, shared the pain of his broken neck during the 1956 Cup Final and now I was cleaning his boots. I would have licked them if he had asked me.

For the first month I called him Mr Trautmann and never found it easy to call him Bert like all the other boys, but really I should have had no fears because he was super to me.

Cliff Sear gained his one and only Welsh Cap against England at Wembley around this time and I gave his boots an extra good luck polish because he was also a grand person and I wanted him to do well.

I didn't get off to a particularly auspicious start in my first week.

I almost crept into the first team dressing-room, brush in hand ready to sweep it out. I'd been at the club since Monday and I don't think half of the players knew I was even there, although I had already been given one valuable piece of advice in how to 'skive' in training. "Make your arms and legs go fast, it makes Jim think you are running fast," I was told. Footballers are obviously smarter than I thought!

This was Friday and the whole of the senior staff were sitting waiting in the dressing-room for news of which eleven had been selected for the first team game the next day.

I was quietly sweeping away when the dressing-room door burst open and in bounced Dave Ewing, the big raw-boned Scottish centre half who had held City's defence together for the past few seasons.

He looked straight at me and snarled in that rasping Scottish voice of his—they used to use Dave's voice to bring the ships in from the River Clyde before he came down to England—"Hey Ginger, what's the team?" I felt my face flush as all the faces of some of the best-known footballers in England focused on me waiting for my reply. I was struggling. I thought I knew all my jobs; boots, baths, sweeping, we even had to wash five lots of kit each Monday by hand, but maybe this was only a Friday job, to the Boss's office, find out the team and come and tell the senior pros.

I played for time, my experience with John Thaw flashing through my mind. "I don't think the Boss has picked it yet," I stuttered praying that I'd come up with a satisfactory answer.

Big Dave looked round at all the lads in bewilderment at my reply and roared "Is he bloody stupid or what?" turned back to me and emphatically tapping his wrist "Fer Chrrist sake, what's the bloody team?"

I couldn't get out of the dressing-room quick enough, and as I left I heard somebody inform him "It's quarter to eleven, Dave".

twelve
LILLESHALL

part one

I was thoroughly enjoying my life as a young footballer. I thought I was playing well and as I walked up the steps to the main entrance of the ground I felt an immense feeling of pride as I reported for work each day.

It was a wonderful feeling to be fit and healthy due to the training and also to be working at something you loved doing; most players feel like this and my advice to them is to savour every moment because it's soon over and there's no turning the clock back.

One of the bonuses of being with a big club like City is that at the end of the season they would send all their best young players for a week's coaching to Lilleshall, where they would be coached by the country's top coaches and also by the England Team Manager, Walter Winterbottom.

This was a first-class idea and it also helped you to meet, mix with and play against the best youngsters from top clubs all over the country.

Lilleshall is a fabulous place for coaching courses. It is a large recreation centre with oak-panelled walls and long corridors with many dormitories for the various teams to sleep in.

It stands in huge acres of grounds and parklands in the little village of Newport, Shropshire, and it possesses every conceivable facility that is required. In fact it was used as a base for the England Squad when we won the World Cup in 1966—all the preparations were done there.

You breathed, ate and slept football for the whole week, and I was glad I was one of the seven boys chosen to represent the club at this prestigious gathering.

The seven days there made a week well spent as far as I was concerned and even in those early days I was watching the coaches perform as closely as I was watching the actual sessions.

I knew the value of having the luck, when you pick a player at random to assist you with your session, to choose a lad who listens and who is capable of demonstrating what you are trying to say, accurately. Because in later years when I was taking my coaching badge examination I was a little put out to be told my subject was goalkeeping, and was really fortunate in my choice of a lad, Keith Coates, who performed heroics for me and finished the session covered from head to toe in mud and glory whilst I passed my examination comfortably. I will always be grateful for his efforts and for my good fortune in picking him.

This particular staff coach, who eventually went on to become Manager of a top First Division club, must have had the same feeling this day when, from a group of players all eager to learn and to assist, he chose me to be his guinea pig.

Now, whilst I was a very nice, willing lad and was prepared to do virtually anything he asked me to ensure the success of his session, I wasn't prepared to allow him, staff coach or not, to make a fool of me in front of 50 of the best young players in England, just to further his own reputation.

The session was to illustrate 'Balance and Control' and after one or two little examples where he would start with the ball perfectly under control, he then invited me to lunge in at him like a wild bull, whereupon he would neatly side step me like a triumphant matador and dribble the ball away.

One or two more little examples like this followed and I dutifully kept diving in and missing both him and the ball. I felt I was being very accommodating, the perfect foil.

However, success seemed to go to his head because he then tried to top the bill with "When I've got the ball under complete control I can do anything I want and you won't be able to stop me".

I nodded, still feeling quite calm and still prepared to be his stooge. He then confronted me perfectly balanced with one foot either side of the ball and proceeded to kneel down, goading me to come and take the ball off him; his plan then was to get to his feet quickly, side step me, dribble the ball away and leave 'the bull' looking even more stupid, which didn't appeal to me at all.

He obviously misjudged my speed off the mark, for no sooner had he invited me to take the ball off him than I covered the necessary few yards and whilst he was kneeling behind the ball whacked it firmly and resoundingly into his bollocks. I smiled a wry smile as he was helped away groaning and trying to find them again. "Only coach what players can do in actual matches," is my moral to that story. His attempt to ridicule me in front of the other players didn't impress the lads one bit, which was illustrated by Tommy Smith's remark when I re-joined him in the group.

"Yer should have gone over the top and squashed 'em." Tommy always believed in going for loose balls, even at sixteen!

There were two main events at Lilleshall, the five-a-side competition with all the teams competing and the big match between the staff and the best eleven players there.

I knew I had absolutely no chance of being selected for this, because it was virtually an England Youth side and I realised as the week went by that there were some really great youngsters there.

I was a bit dubious about my chances in the five-a-side as well because there were seven of us and you don't need to be a mathematician to work out that two of us were going to be unlucky, and as I was the most junior player there it was odds on I was going to be one of the lads to miss out.

I had already resigned myself to this when Johnny Hart,

who was in charge of us, came to our dormitory to announce his selection to represent Manchester City in this big competition.

As I expected, I was not in it, but included in the team was Alan Baker.

Alan Baker was a great little inside forward who had, the previous year, been the star of the England Schoolboys team. A smashing lad, who, during the week was great mates with me and the rest of the lads, and spent nearly all his time in our dormitory. The only problem was ..... he played for Aston Villa!

"John, how the hell can he play for us when he plays for Aston Villa," I steamed in, "it's not as though we are short of players, there's three of us here who would give anything to play." But John was adamant and flatly refused to change his mind.

I looked hard at him, I was only very young and daren't have told him what I thought of him at that moment, or I would have been on the next train home.

I went back to the other two lads who had been left out, Neil Young and Roy Thurnham, and told them I was going to do something about it.

Along the hallowed corridors I went, up to the imposing door and knocked quietly.

"Come in," a posh voice said. I entered the private quarters of the now Sir Walter Winterbottom, England Team Manager and supremo, and enquired if it were permissable for a five-a-side team called "Fred's Gang" to enter the competition alongside Arsenal, Aston Villa, Manchester City, Manchester United and all the other giants.

I reasoned there must somewhere be two other unlucky lads who had not been selected for their respective clubs and would fancy playing for my team, therefore enabling them to play in the competition.

Mr Winterbottom chuckled, thought about it, but finally agreed, so my team were entered; now I had only to find two players.

I went to each bedroom in turn, but most of the clubs had

only brought five players with them so they were all selected for their rightful clubs.

Finally I acquired a Scottish lad, Ian Cairns from Aston Villa, and eventually came across Barry Gould, a centre forward from Arsenal. Barry was keen to play, but his enthusiasm waned a little when I told him he had to play in goal; still it was a game, so he played in goal.

We settled down in the auditorium to watch the competition commence and I was immediately struck by the lack of organisation by most of the teams.

Our own team, Manchester City, including guest star Alan Baker, were unceremoniously eliminated in the first round, and before our first game I called a hurried team talk in our bedroom.

In view of the fact that we were 'so inferior' I thought we stood a better chance if we had a set plan. So I instructed big Roy Thurnham to patrol our own goal area, so cutting down the number of shots poor Barry might have to save, told Neil Young to do no graft (he was delighted to hear this) but to stay right up front and to remember his shooting boots, and that Ian Cairns and I would do all the work; that I thought would be a better bet than everybody just chasing aimlessly around the gym as most of the others seemed to be doing.

In the second round we comfortably disposed of Southampton, the conquerors of the Manchester City team ..... plus of course Alan Baker, and then went on through the various rounds to beat, much to Ian Cairn's delight, Aston Villa in the final ..... minus of course Alan Baker.

Throughout the competition we scored 23 goals and every single one of them was scored by Neil Young. He appreciated the hard work we had all put in, of course, but it was a tremendous achievement on his part and it was with a feeling of great pride and self-satisfaction that I led my team, 'Fred's Gang', up to receive our trophy and medals from Joe Mercer, ironically manager of the defeated finalists, Aston Villa, and even more ironically the man for whom, in the future, Neil would win the F.A. Cup.

As we left the arena I couldn't help a sly glance towards where the City lads were sat with Johnny and, of course ..... Alan Baker.

part two

The following year we were back again, only this time I was a more senior player. John was in charge of us again, and when the subject of the five-a-side competition was raised, John asked me "Who do you want in your team?" Now that was a bit more like it, I like a man who learns from his mistakes!

So after deciding to stick with my 'master plan' of the previous year, I plumped for Big Mike Batty to do the 'area patrol', Neil to do the same job as last year, with Ken Fletcher and I doing the donkey work. We again didn't have a keeper so we persuaded Derek Floyd to go in goal.

All the big clubs were as disorganised as before and we walked through all the rounds to beat Bristol Rovers 4-1 in the final to prove last year's effort was not a fluke. Neil, just for a change, scoring all the four goals.

We scored seventeen goals this time round. I nipped in with three as did Ken Fletcher, with Neil having a very subdued time by only scoring eleven out of the seventeen goals; he must be slipping!

To crown a very rewarding week I captained the Best XI team against the staff, marking Welsh International Phil Woosnam, now Commissioner of The North American Soccer League of Football in America, and received a personalised coaching book from Walter Winterbottom to mark the occasion.

See you in a couple of years Walter when you present me with my first England Cap!

thirteen

A PROFESSIONAL AT LAST – LYING DOWN ON THE JOB

My success at Lilleshall must have reached the ears of the Boss. Thank you, John! because the week after I returned home I was signed as a full-time professional ..... £10 per week, my mates got £12!

No more boots to clean, only my own. Even though I was now in order to let my former apprentice colleagues do them, I insisted on looking after them myself.

Things were going quite well, the Youth Cup Team, of which I was the captain, was quietly progressing through the rounds.

Leeds with Gary Sprake, Paul Reaney, Jimmy Greenhoff, Terry Cooper etc, were accounted for 3-1, Neil converting a couple of my crosses for two good goals.

Nearly a slip up in the second round, however, when we were two goals down to Burnley at Turf Moor. Willie Morgan was having an inspired day on the right wing for them and we were finding it difficult to cope. However, we managed to peg goals back from Neil Young (who else!) and one from Glyn Pardoe to equal the score.

It was a tremendous game, end to end stuff with neither side prepared to concede an inch.

In the dying minutes I picked up a ball and ran it at the Burnley defence. As a wall of claret and blue converged on me, I slid on my back and managed to set Neil free with a toe poke pass whilst at full stretch; from my prostrate position on the ground I watched as Neil's usually trusty left foot hammered the ball ..... wide of the goal.

Such was my disappointment that whilst I lay there flat out I put my hands to my head and lay with supressed despair that this final effort had gone unrewarded, not an unusual reaction.

Two seconds later I was back on my feet racing into position to commence battle, and indeed from the resultant goal kick it was my header which sent Glyn Pardoe free to score his second and winning goal.

We all went berserk, and about fifteen seconds later after the final whistle had signalled a fine victory we danced back to the dressing-room.

What a game!

We were still jubilant as we prepared to enjoy our well-earned bath. Johnny Hart was praising our never-say-die spirit when the dressing-room door burst open and in strode the Vice-Chairman.

Albert Alexander was a tiny, spritely old gentleman with silver hair and a piercing voice; we mortals hardly ever saw him but he seemed a nice man to me.

He stood in the doorway, looked round at all the happy perspiring faces and immediately singled me out.

"You!" he pointed his finger at me accusingly, "were shattered—I've never in my life seen a Manchester City player lie down during a game before," he went on.

"Mister Alexander," interrupted John in an attempt to defend me from this ridiculous and totally unwarranted attack; he made it sound as though I had brought out a couple of pillows and had a kip in the penalty area, but little Albert wouldn't be deterred. "I'm going to report to the Manager that you are in need of extra training and I'll make sure you get it." With that final blast he turned on his little heels and left.

"Forget it," said John, but I knew that would be easier said than done and I hoped he wouldn't be there for the next round against the old enemy Manchester United at Old Trafford.

We went into this game feeling very confident—over confident as it turned out—because we had beaten them twice in previous months.

It was a particularly nostalgic night for me because my old school pal Bob Smith was captain of United that night, and after we tossed up in front of 15,000 people, quite a big crowd for a Youth match, we stood together in the centre circle while the teams changed ends and arranged to see each other in 'The Plaza' after the game. Ducie Avenue seemed a million miles away.

We played terrible; I had a diabolical game, got myself booked for a foul on Alan Duff, which wasn't really like me at all, and we thoroughly deserved to lose three nil.

My performance in this showpiece game was a big disappointment to me, and as I trudged away from the visitors' dressing-room past the home team's, I glanced through the little window in the door and the only thing I could see was Bob zipping up his pants and preparing himself to meet me in 'The Plaza'. I decided to give it a miss.

'The Plaza' was our meeting place. Bob and I were regular visitors both at lunch-time and some evenings. It was a dance hall on Oxford Street in Manchester. Apparently it had been quite an ordinary sort of place for a number of years, but I only remember it from when Jimmy Savile swept in and transformed the place. Now it was the rendezvous for all the young people around Manchester and the idea of lunch-time musical interludes and snacks with DJs like Dave Lee Travis playing records for an admission of sixpence for two hours was a winner. What value and what good clean fun.

We never used to dance; Bob fancied himself as a bit of a mover but never really got the chance to prove it. We sat just listening to the music and chatting, all the City players used to go each lunch-time, but Bob was usually the only United player.

After lunch, if I didn't go back training, four of us, Derek Panter, Paul Aimson, Bob and myself would spend the afternoon either playing table tennis in the YMCA or at the pictures. Our stature as footballers gained us free admittance to either place and even though there was a sneaking thought at the back of my mind that the afternoons could be put to better use, life was idyllic and free from worry. It would all change soon enough.

fourteen

JOBS FOR THE BOYS

The close season is when the stars take a break and recharge their batteries for the next season but for the youngsters it's a chance to earn extra money.

The club still paid us of course during the summer, but with almost three months off some of us looked for part-time jobs.

The previous year I had helped my Dad in the butcher's shop, and learned the first lesson in the art of butchering, if you knock the knife off the block don't catch it!

I learned this lesson the hard way. I was boning out a huge piece of meat on my first day, my reflexes were ultra sharp as I just managed to catch the razor sharp knife by the blade before it hit the sawdusted floor. I stood there amazed at my own stupidity as it dug into my hand, blood oozing through my fingers ..... and the coldness, they didn't need a deep freeze in that shop. I don't know how my Dad could stand it ..... it wasn't the life for me.

That year the four of us decided we would get a vigorous, outdoor, healthy job.

We would perform outdoor tasks and return for pre-season training, bronzed (or in my case red and freckly) and raring to go.

Thus, we four willing hands reported for duty at 8 am to Fog Lane Park, a large park in South Manchester where I had actually played many times for Ducie Avenue, to start work as council gardeners.

I had never lifted a finger in our garden at home. I thought hydrangeas were a Scottish football team. Bob, who lived next door to Gosling's Fish Shop on Moston Lane, didn't even have a garden, neither did Paul in Landseer Street, Salford. Derek lived in a nice house in Chorlton but being the sort of lad he was he only slept in his garden.

We all volunteered for 'hedging' on our first day; we thought it might just be within our capabilities.

We were expected to trim the hedges of the whole park in one day. We managed about a hundred yards between the four of us as we joined in a game with some kids, with the traditional coats down for goals.

This became a regular daily event, developing into a series comparable with the World Cup as word got round the neighbourhood, and it was inevitable that we would be hauled before the boss, 'Washy', and told to buck our ideas up.

To remove us from the temptations of games of football, we were transferred to a housing estate in Hattersley, near Hyde, to mow the lawns of old people who couldn't mow them for themselves.

The old people loved having four footballers to chat to and spoiled us with coffee, sandwiches and the odd shandy and in return for their kindness, never got their lawns mowed; again we were summoned by 'Washy' for another warning.

Soon after this we should have been on weeding, but the old bandstand with a double seat across the middle provided us with an ideal head-tennis court and soon a very serious competition was in progress; Paul and I were locked in a close doubles game with Derek and Bob, when I heard a rustle in the bushes. It was 'Washy' spying on us, but it was a crucial point in the game and because he hadn't revealed himself I decided to say nothing about his presence to the others.

The game continued. "OUT!" shouted Bob, whose motto in life is "If at first you don't succeed ..... cheat!" "A mile in," said Paul. "Definitely out," insisted Bob desperate to win at all costs. "Come off it Bob." The argument raged, one saying 'in" the other saying "out".

In the end I thought of the only fair thing to do so I turned to the bushes and said:

"You saw it all sir, was it in or was it out?"

'Washy' stormed out of the bushes and we were immediately back in his office for a final warning.

The end was near, however, because two days later we were in the pub at lunch-time, playing snooker and we simply did not go back that day.

I don't know what got into us, because basically we were nice, harmless lads, from good families; but being footballers we just couldn't settle into doing menial jobs even for three months, and I left, with 'Washy's' words rattling round my head.

"None of you will ever make anything of your lives if you don't make it at football ..... especially you," he said prodding me in the chest.

So with a green card with "Never to work for the Manchester Corporation again" stamped on the bottom in my pocket, we left the employment of the Parks Department of Manchester Corporation.

Thank goodness I'll never have to work for a living! I thought.

fifteen

ENTER MISS TUCKER

Season 1962 was the one I hoped would see my big break-through. I had already made my debut for the reserves.

Even this wasn't straightforward. I had been selected for the 'A' team ..... again! when Harry Godwin came to our house and told me Barney McDonald (another non-wing half who had been switched recently into my position to block it even further) had gone down with 'flu during the night and I was his replacement for the game at Stoke.

I thought I did well in a four nil victory and even though I received the usual yawn from Fred Tilson at the end of the game I was heartened by the fact that the experienced George Hannah (he actually scored the third and killer goal for New-castle when they beat City in the Cup Final, but I had long since forgiven him because he was a smashing fellow), Scottish International Jackie Plenderleith, and winger Ray Sambrook all made it their business to say how well they thought I'd done and looking at them closely I think they meant it and weren't just being kind.

Came the following Friday, mine was the only name missing from the team sheet, even the normally hard Barney McDonald came and apologised to me for taking my place.

I hung about a bit after everybody had gone home expecting Fred to give me a "You did alright, son, but ....." sort of explanation, but nothing.

This sort of non-communication I have now come to accept as a normal part of the game, but have never been able to understand the reasoning behind it.

Shortly afterwards my nightschool pal Malcolm Darlington (we enrolled together in the Moss House woodwork class and were both very adept at making sawdust), a left winger with a flair for goalscoring, was named in the squad for the away game at 'Spurs.

"Debut for Darlington" was the headline in the 'Evening Chronicle'. "Darlington Plays" quoted another paper.

On arriving at White Hart Lane all the players, including Malcolm, went to inspect the pitch. On returning to the dressing-room, as is customary, all the kit was laid out by numbers with the boots of whoever is wearing each set of kit alongside it. Malcolm's boots were still in the skip, so he assumed he wasn't playing as all the other players began to strip.

All day Friday, the evening at the hotel, Saturday morning, the game and the journey home not a word was said to him. He is the boss of a big building society now in Northampton and whenever I see him I always ask him "Has the Boss told you whether you're playing against 'Spurs yet?" It's always my first greeting and we have a good laugh about it ..... now.

One manager said to me before a game "I'm leaving you out today, because you played well last week at Barrow". "Oh? really ..... thanks very much."

Another one sent for me, and whilst I was standing there wondering what was coming next, he actually took off his shoe, peered inside it and said "I've got a nail coming through my bloody shoe, I'm dropping you today", all in one breath without once taking his nose out of his shoe.

"Cobblers!" I replied ..... "Take it to the cobblers," I went on quietly as he looked up at me, "and then place me on the transfer list." I couldn't play for a spineless manager like that.

"Be honest with me," that's all I've ever wanted from Managers or coaches and it's what I've always tried to be with my players.

They can say what they like about me ..... but they cannot

say I'm not honest. Things got so bad at City at the time, they even brought in a hypnotist to hypnotise the players. The spectators thought they were already under the influence.

The season also turned into a nightmare for me, culminating in my subsequent free transfer. So I didn't captain England whilst at Manchester City, but my innersoles did!

Just before I left, there was an England friendly match played at Maine Road and Bobby Moore was complaining about his boots and asked for a pair of innersoles. None could be found, so I graciously nipped to the bootroom and gave him mine from out of my own boots.

I can't understand how those innersoles could play so badly the previous Saturday yet play so well for England, they must simply have possessed the big match temperament!

As Bobby climbed the steps to the Royal Box a couple of years later on the greatest day in English football history, to receive the World Cup from the Queen, I wondered if he was still wearing my innersoles!

The only redeeming feature about this particular period was that a little bit of romance entered my life.

I used to go out at weekends with the City lads and Bob, but really only for the company and a change of environment, and actually enjoyed a couple of hours entertainment at lunch-times just as much.

Females were quite a way down my list of priorities, which obviously had football at the top of it and saving up for a little car a close second.

'The Plaza' was still the number-one haunt at lunch-time, but a little coffee bar in Lloyd Street was making quite a name for itself since the "Under new management" sign had appeared.

It was called 'The Oasis' and it was clean and well run. They served a handsome cup of coffee, and they didn't let any riff-raff in — "a directive from the owner".

The owner was a certain Ric Dixon, a short stocky young man, who stood no messing from anybody and who soon gained himself a reputation as a hard-headed businessman who knew exactly what he wanted and made sure nobody stopped him from getting it, and he ran 'The Oasis' in a firm and business-like manner. His attention to detail made all his customers feel comfortable because he made sure they came first.

He introduced local pop groups to 'The Oasis' and they made the lunch-time sessions go with a swing and it was a worthy challenger to 'Jimmy Savile's Plaza'.

The Beatles played there for a fiver, between them, Gary Glitter, or Paul Raven as he was then known, for half that; 'The Hollies' were big favourites, also. 'Freddie and the Dreamers', who were in later years to make me Captain and honorary member of their football team, I played dozens of games for them and helped to raise a lot of money for various charities. Great lads. Herman's Hermits also featured; one of the group, Lek, and I had our coats pinched one lunch-time— definitely not 'The Oasis' image, and Mr Dixon scoured Manchester to make sure they were recovered.

Freddie Starr and the Delmonts, Gerry and the Pacemakers, Billy J. Kramer, Wayne Fontana and the Mindbenders, you name them, Mr Dixon introduced them to Manchester, and it's little wonder that he went on to become one of show business's top impresarios handling the careers of some of the world's top recording stars.

This lunch-time I was sitting in his establishment with Neil Young, sipping our frothy coffee, listening to 'The Hollies' and generally surveying the scene.

My eye fell upon a pretty dark haired young thing with enormous eyes and nice legs and I watched as she fluttered about the place. She never kept still; finally she went behind the counter of the bar and poured herself a cup of coffee— what a nerve!

"Who's the girl in blue?" I asked Neil, who by now was becoming an authority on any female in Manchester and the outlying districts between the ages of sixteen and twenty-one.

"She's the owner's sister-in-law, her name is Judith Tucker, she works opposite the YMCA on Peter Street in a travel agency. She used to go to Ladybarn School and she hasn't got a boyfriend," was Neil's quick synopsis. I knew he wouldn't let me down.

I watched her for a few more lunch-times and decided it was about time she made my acquaintance. I asked her to dance, definitely not one of my strong points, and then let her know that it would be quite acceptable to me if she wished to take me to the pictures. She admired my cheek and we began to go out regularly together after that.

The poor girl didn't know what she was letting herself in for.

"Dad, this is Fred, he's in the process of getting the sack from Manchester City, he can hardly walk due to an injury, so the prospects of him getting fixed up with a new club are remote, apart from football he's never done a day's work in his life." Hardly the ideal introduction to a future son-in-law, but that was about the size of it, so it was no use trying to disguise it.

Judith even in those early days was a great support to me; I needed all I could get! She, along with my Mam and Dad, kept reassuring me "A club will have seen you play before your injury so don't worry, I'm sure something will turn up". But as I went to Maine Road for the last time to collect my boots, I already felt out of place, a stranger. Nothing had turned up. The only person I saw that day was Glyn Pardoe. He wished me good luck and I left with my boots in my hand, a feeling of emptiness in my stomach.

Where do I go from here?

sixteen

THE LINCOLN IMP

We were well into the summer of '63, and very little was moving. Especially me.

My leg was healing, but slowly. It seemed that every flag on the pavement was a potential trap as I always seemed to find the uneven one and stub my toe, as I shuffled along. Every kerbstone I inevitably twisted on, setting my progress back a few days. Whenever something is sore you always manage to bang it.

I had received one or two tentative offers of trials ..... that dreaded word ..... trial. I know how Martin Bormann felt! But I was a fully fledged pro now and I didn't think I should be having trials. "They either want me or they don't," I reasoned, but in reality in my situation I wasn't really in a position to argue.

My summer holiday, a long awaited sojurn to Butlins with Bob Smith and Dave Latham of United and our pal Peter Podmore, ironically one of my assailants with John Thaw in my Ducie days, was nearly upon me and I really was hoping to get my future sorted out before we four ex-Ducie boys hit the high spots of Pwllheli. An offer of a trial at Preston North End, good club I thought, but a trial! An offer of a trial at Chesterfield. If it's to be a trial it might as well be Preston rather than Chesterfield. An offer of a full contract ..... I don't believe it ..... Runcorn ..... "Don't think me disrespectful," I said to their Manager Jack Boothway on the 'phone, "but Run who? are they an Irish team? Thanks very much for your offer, I'll let you know.''

In a couple more years I would get to know Runcorn and many more non-league teams very well.

An offer of a contract with Port Elizabeth in South Africa; but I didn't think I'd be able to get home for my dinner, so I declined with thanks, and finally two offers of Fourth Division Football from Workington and Lincoln City; both arrived on the same day.

A quick check on the map revealed they were both approximately the same distance from Manchester, but the name of Lincoln painted a more promising picture for me so I arranged to travel down there to meet the Manager and have a look round.

Workington Manager Ken Furphy had a narrow escape that day!

As this was yet another big day for me, my Dad took his second day off work in 30 years and drove me the 90-odd miles to Lincoln.

Lincoln is a lovely city with the Cathedral perched high on the hill lording it majestically over all else; it is the focal point of everything and its Roman Arches and olde worlde charm really impressed me. Everybody seemed to travel on bikes or on foot and the pace of things was quite leisurely.

These were my first impressions as we had a quick tour of the city before making our way to Sincil Bank.

We arrived at the ground just before lunch-time, much to the displeasure of the Manager, who had been waiting for me at the railway station the whole time.

I was sitting in his cluttered little office under the stand when he stamped in, far from pleased. ''He's not bothered to turn up,'' I heard him say to his trainer Bill McGlen. Before Bill had time to reply he opened the door and entered his office.

I hadn't told him I was coming by train so didn't feel an apology was necessary on my part, but instinctively I felt that I didn't like Mr Bill Anderson at all.

I should have heeded my sixth sense and left there and then to take my chance at Workington, but in those days my intuition, which over the years has been developed to a fine art, was still in its infancy and I didn't have the confidence in it that I have now. So I sat tight and waited to see what would happen next.

First of all I had to pass the scrutiny of his Labrador dog, Sandy; no easy task because I think he thought I was a bone! and I felt sure he would try and bury me any minute.

Unknown to me Sandy was the most influential individual at Sincil Bank—if he liked you, you were OK. The lads firmly believed Sandy drew up the retained list at the end of the season.

He eventually turned away disdainfully and now it was Mr Anderson's turn to cast his eye over me, literally. Bill, a bachelor, was a big man, overweight, with one eye that had a mind of its own and seemed to swivel and turn whenever it felt like it. I was never quite sure whether he was talking to me or not, a most unlikely looking Manager.

This time, however, I knew I was on safe ground because I was the only person in the room as he said:

"You are a bit scrawny, but we'll soon build you up here. I've already spoken to your landlady and told her she must give you two pints of milk a day and she has to feed you a steak this thick every single day," he said holding his fingers at least two inches apart.

It sounded like star treatment to me but still I wasn't sure. The city was beautiful, the ground was in good condition, the Club seemed sound, the prospects bright, trainer Bill McGlen an admirable fellow, a promise of steaks two inches thick every day, what was the problem ..... the nagging doubt was The Manager.

I left with a promise that I would "think it over" whilst I was on holiday the following week.

I set off for the delights of North Wales with the boys in fine spirits, but still a little dubious, also the problem of my leg was still nagging me. It was a few months since the injury and I hadn't run a step or kicked a ball since—would I still be able to play and also in the circumstances would I be cheating any team that signed me. These thoughts were in my mind as the train chugged out of Manchester Exchange Station.

Any worries I had were soon forgotten, however, when we arrived at the camp. We teamed up with four Swansea players including Welsh International winger Barrie Jones, two Port Vale players, Terry Alcock later to play for many years for Blackpool and Portland Timbers and Micky Porter, plus two Tranmere Rovers lads, Dave Roberts and Dave Russell, and we had a great week.

It was at the height of the revelry that Bill Anderson played his trump card that really pricked my vanity. He had learned a trick or two in his nineteen years as a Manager, one of which was that a player's weak spot is his ego.

We were all quietly sunbathing, planning our onslaught for the evening when the tannoy system rang out loud and clear. "Will Mr Fred Eyre please report to the main reception?"

"This must be important," I said as Bob and I galloped to the reception. I was gasping when I got there, I was so much out of condition, and breathlessly took the 'phone which was being offered to me by a beaming Redcoat.

"Have you made your mind up yet?" It was Bill Anderson.

"Well not really," I stalled.

"I'll tell you what I'll do, I'll send the forms all filled in just requiring your signature by special delivery, then if you decide, simply sign them and send them back, and remember I've told your landlady ..... two inches thick."

Sure enough the very next day the forms arrived and I called a board meeting of all the Swansea lads and included the think tank of Tranmere Rovers, Port Vale, Manchester United and Old Mostonians, Pete Podmore's team, and it was unanimously decided that Bill obviously wanted me so desperately that it would be very ungracious of me to deprive him of my talents.

So on 3rd July 1963 at 12.40 pm at Butlins Holiday Camp in Pwllheli, North Wales, in Chalet number EB17 to be precise, I signed for Lincoln City. I became an IMP.

It was an ironic place to sign ..... I went from one holiday camp to another.

seventeen

WELCOME TED EYRE

My preparations were almost complete. I had my cases packed as I prepared to leave home; there was just one little thing I needed to do, I wanted to treat myself to a scrapbook.

I had always craved for a proper News Cutting Book but had always put off buying one ..... probably because I didn't have any press cuttings to stick in it!

Now with a bit more publicity imminent I decided to splash out and buy one. "You'll get one at any commercial stationers," I was told, so I journeyed into town, bid a hero's farewell to 'The Plaza' and 'Oasis' and set about finding a 'commercial stationers'. I tried four such emporiums without success and had just about given up when I stumbled across a tiny stationer's shop on the corner of Booth Street as I cut through towards Spring Gardens to get my bus in Piccadilly.

I didn't hold out much hope as I went down the few narrow stairs into the basement shop. I was in luck. "Thank you," I said as the assistant put my purchase in a bag. "You are the only shop in Manchester with these scrapbooks." When I eventually bought this very shop just a few years later I made sure we were never out of stock of newscutting books!

I left the premises highly pleased with my purchase but not as pleased as I was to be with my purchase in the future.

"Look after your money," were my Mother's tearful instructions as I left for the train to Lincoln this sunny Wednesday lunch-time.

A new life lay ahead. I was upset to see my Mother so distressed at the departure of her only child but what could I do ..... I had to prove Manchester City wrong and I had to start again somewhere.

"Look after your money," I thought, and chuckled to myself at my Mam's fussiness as I sat on the train to Sheffield, where I had to change, pick up the train to Retford and finally another train from there to Lincoln.

"There's not much danger that I wouldn't look after it," I thought. I'd drawn every penny I had in the world out of the bank and I tapped my inside pocket to make sure my wallet was still there.

"Nearly there," I thought, "another half an hour, I'll nip down to the toilet and spruce myself up in case there's a civic reception."

Must look my best.

A quick wash, a comb of the locks, where's my comb? in my wallet, ah yes!

"Handsome brute"—back to my seat to complete the journey.

"Lincoln," came the guard's loud voice. "I'd better get my ticket ready, it's in my wallet."

Never have I had a feeling like the feeling I got at that moment ..... empty, my God! Every penny that I possessed in the world gone, away from home and with not a penny to my name.

I flew back down the corridor to the little toilet, threw open the door and there it was lying there, in all its glory. Thank goodness there were no people on board that day with weak bladders.

I grabbed my precious wallet, stuffed all my money into my back pocket, emptied the rest of its contents into my jacket pocket and promptly threw the wallet away and have never used one since. I don't intend to experience that feeling ever again.

By the time I'd trekked to the ground from the station with

my cases my arms felt as long as King Kong's, but I was certainly looking forward to the two-inch thick steak that had been organised for me.

Three other 'big' signings had already arrived when I trooped into Bill Anderson's office. He immediately sent for trainer Bill McGlen. Bill was a trainer in the old mould, big old-fashioned football boots, his trousers tucked into his stockings, and wearing an old maroon tracksuit top with a muffler. He was a Geordie who had played wing half for Manchester United. I'd seen him play at Old Trafford and later for Oldham Athletic before coming to 'The Imps' to work for Bill Anderson. He was a super, honest, hard-working man who loved the game.

"This is our new signing, Ted Eyre." Mr Anderson introduced me to Bill. "Pleased to meet you, Ted, son" said Bill in his Geordie accent.

"Actually it's Fred ..... Fred Eyre," I quickly corrected, a feeling of foreboding spreading through my body. He looked unsuccessfully around his cluttered desk for an ashtray to knock the ash off his cigar. Bill McGlen obligingly offered his cupped hand for the Manager to deposit his ash, and Mr Anderson promptly responded to this gesture by grinding the burning cigar stub into the palm of Bill's hand, while Bill bravely stood there gritting his teeth.

"Take him round the town and try to find him somewhere to live" ..... he dismissed us both with a flick of his podgy hand without raising his one eye from the desk. The other one could probably see me quite clearly from that angle. I never could see eye to eye with Bill right from the start!

I dutifully picked up my cases and followed Bill out into the streets of Lincoln and we traipsed round the cobbled streets in an attempt to find a roof over my head.

I was a little perplexed. The Manager had, he said, already organised two pints of milk a day and a two-inch thick steak with my landlady, so what was I doing being hawked around Lincoln like this.

In the end I decided to take the 'Bill by the horns' and said to him, "Bill, what's going on, what about mi' steak?"

"Mi' steak, son," he said "it's the biggest mistake you'll ever make coming here"!

How right he was.

eighteen

RESCUED
BY MR & MRS FOLEY

Thankfully somebody took pity on the poor wretch and offered me a home, actually double pity because she also took in one of the other signings, Bobby Murray, a former Scottish schoolboy international who had just been released from West Bromwich Albion.

Mr & Mrs Foley were kindness itself to me and I settled down immediately in their terraced house at number 17 Pennell Street.

It was situated amongst the many streets surrounding the ground and the river ran past the house at the foot of the garden alongside the outside toilet.

Jim Foley was a grand man. He looked to be getting on a bit even then, but I never knew his actual age because he had a young mind and we were both on the same wavelength and enjoyed a good laugh together.

He had experienced a rough time in the war which maybe aged him a bit, he was in the Air Force and was always regaling me with stories of how he helped Churchill to win the war.

Whenever there was a flash of the great man on TV I would always shout to him "Here's your mate Winnie on the telly," and he would say that he looked just the same, he hadn't changed from their days in action together.

The times that Churchill appeared on TV showing his famous two-finger sign to the world I would get Jim going by saying,

"Look, two fingers, it's his way of telling everybody that he didn't do it all by himself, that there were two of you involved, but you're just too modest to boast about it".

Jim now worked at Scampton, the Air Force base in Lincolnshire. He was also the Vernons pools collector for the camp, and because Jim couldn't drive I took him round the camp every Friday night to collect the pools money.

We would start about seven o'clock and sing all the old songs together until we returned home about nine o'clock.

Our favourite was 'Swanee' and I sang the song while he harmonised in his thick scouse accent. In fact, we were in full song the night President Kennedy was shot. When we heard the sad news it was one of the few nights we completed the journey in silence. A fine man was Jim.

All the while we were teaching his wife Jenny to drive, but inexplicably she kept failing her test. Jim would, after each failure, criticise the examiner. "My Aunt Kate had more idea than him," was one of his favourite expressions and I still say it to this day.

On the day of Jenny's latest attempt Jim was supremely confident that she would pass at last.

He arrived home at tea time with an expectant look on his face. "Well?" he said. "Failed," said Jenny miserably, and I literally rolled off the settee with mirth as Jim ceremoniously took off his hat, threw it onto the lounge floor in disgust, and proceeded to jump up and down on it with both feet with pent up rage, finishing with a shot Bobby Charlton would have been proud of as the poor hat was propelled into the fire.

Good old Jim.

His wife Jenny was a kind person who did and indeed still does a lot of charity work. She was a good cook, who used to give us breakfasts of such proportions that I had to ask her for just a piece of toast because I was finding it hard to train after such a feast. Her cooking was always first class but the same cannot be said of Jim's. He deputised one day and absent-mindedly made me a cup of coffee with gravy powder instead of Nescafe ..... Aagh Bisto!

She was much younger than Jim and he was very proud of her, but the light of his life was his son Michael who was about seven or eight. He looked upon me as an elder brother and I used to play 'Cluedo' and 'Monopoly' with him for nights on end during the long winter evenings in front of the fire.

I now realise how he always beat me at Monopoly because now he is one of the country's top financial experts running the finances of one of Britain's largest companies in Geneva, so really I had no chance.

I spent one Christmas in the Foley household. Bob Murray had long since departed due to a slight altercation with Jim one evening, and on Christmas Eve Michael was safely tucked up in bed as we slowly and quietly crept up the stairs loaded up with Michael's Christmas presents.

"Ssh, follow me," said Jim, who was a bit dodgy on his pins at the best of times, his carpet-slippered feet slithering across the lino. "Be as quiet as you can," he warned as he eased open the bedroom door to reveal Michael's angelic face in a state of slumber.

"Not a sound," he said as he juggled with his arms full of presents.

"Crash"!! The bang and rustle of paper nearly wóke the street as I looked down at Jim, lying flat out on the bedroom floor, presents scattered everywhere. Jim had tripped over the wire from the electric blanket.

"Father Christmas asked me to give you this Michael," he said from his outstretched position as he handed a bemused Michael the only Christmas present he had left in his hand. I slid down the wall convulsed again, not many people could make me laugh like Jim.

So it was these good people who took me in and I stayed with them the whole time I was in Lincoln. I trained during the day and in the early evening I nipped down to the ground after the Manager had gone home, to dip my leg into a wax bath they had there. It seemed to do it good, you keep dipping it in and out of the red hot wax until after about an hour your leg is like a giant candle, then you sit and hope something good is happening inside.

Some evenings I borrowed Jenny's car, which, because neither of them could drive, was stuck outside all day and I would drive to the coast, Skegness or Sutton-on-Sea, and paddle for hours in the freezing sea in the hope that the briny would help my leg to heal.

After a few weeks of this it began to feel stronger and I was quite looking forward to the first game of the season. Unfortunately Bob Murray had broken his toe, so he was feeling sorry for himself because he now had his leg encased in plaster.

I liked Bob, we got on well together and he revelled in his reputation as a tight Scotsman. The usual thing had happened, I signed for £14 per week, he was on £18, and after he had paid Mrs Foley his plan was whatever he had left in shillings and pence from his wages, say he drew £13 16s.9d, he would discipline himself to live the week on the odd 16s.9d. All the pounds would go into the bank. I don't know where he is today but I'll bet he's a millionaire!

This was the night before my all-important first game and Bob's girl friend, Heather, arrived from West Bromwich to see him. There wasn't another spare bed so Bob with his plastered leg moved into my bed and gallantly gave Heather his. I spent the whole night dodging his leg as he struggled for comfort, I was feeling far from refreshed for the big kick-off next day.

The season moved along slowly and I could tell I was getting nowhere fast. In this time I received two pieces of advice from Bill McGlen, "When you get older son the penny will drop," he told me. Again I didn't comprehend, but he has turned out to be right. As I got older I saw the whole picture crystal clearly, the bad coaches and Managers, how to work around them rather than work against them. Moves on the field, I would see three or four in advance of everybody else.

The penny dropped, but too late for me ..... the real secret is for it to drop early.

The other piece of advice was more direct and to the point, "Why don't you pack it in, go home, get yourself a job and play part-time?''

"Pack in ..... never! throw the towel in ..... no chance!"

He certainly knew a thing or two did Bill McGlen.

Ken Bracewell, a very experienced full-back from Burnley, was my pal. He used to look after me, and he told me to stay in the game as long as I could. "When the dressing-room door closes the factory door opens for me," he said. "Make sure it isn't the same for you."

I intended to heed his advice.

nineteen

ALL CHANGE AT CREWE

The season spluttered on. About half-way through my leg 'conked out' again, though not as serious this time. I was back in action after fourteen weeks and managed a few games before the end of the season, but another free transfer was a certainty as the season drew to its close.

Such was the inevitability of the situation that when Jim crept into my bedroom one morning and solemnly handed me a registered letter with 'Lincoln City Football Club' printed on the front, I drowsily took it from him, pushed it under my pillow and went back to sleep. It was, in all honesty, a relief to be released.

My situation was even bleaker than the previous year as I bade farewell to Mr & Mrs Foley and young Michael, who had not been to sleep all the previous night because he was so upset at my impending departure. Three hours later I was back home, things again hadn't gone according to plan, but I had a few good memories, my new scrapbook had quite a few cuttings stuck in.

"Will Lincoln be at full strength today ..... or will Eyre play?"

That made good reading whilst I was having my breakfast.

"Fred Eyre, a very reliable defender ..... he always turns up on time," was another beauty.

"The Manager has switched Eyre from right half to left half to make room for the return of Murray; it makes no difference to the two-footed Eyre, who can play equally badly on either side.''

They just don't write them like that any more.

"Well, where do I go from here?" I said pensively to my Dad.

He suggested writing to a couple of clubs asking for a trial .... Bloody trial, I hated the very sound of the word, but I was certain nobody would come for me and I was right.

I wrote off to one club giving my details and finished off the letter by saying "Can I have a trial?" They wrote back and simply said:

"No you can't."

I think it was can't!

Then from out of the blue came the offer of a trial with Huddersfield Town. That would do me nicely, second division, a step up of two divisions and I could still live at home.

I trained on my own throughout the summer and reported to Leeds Road feeling in tip-top condition, and did well from the start, with promising lads like Frank Worthington, Chris Catlin and Derek Parkin. They were fine young players and I enjoyed linking up with them in training.

After five weeks at Huddersfield the 'old war wound' let me down again and I was forced to report to physiotherapist Roy Goodall, who treated me for a fortnight and then put a report in to the Manager, Eddie Boot, who sent for me later in the day.

"I'm sorry, but we'll have to pay you up son. Our advice to you is to quit the game for a year, give your leg a chance to get better and if you want to come back in a year you are more than welcome."

Eddie Boot was a gentleman, and in my heart I had a feeling he was right, but a year! The thought was unbearable. I said goodbye to trainer Ian Greaves but couldn't face the lads for some reason. I nipped into the dressing-room to get my gear (have boots, will travel). The only person there was Derek Parkin, who has been Wolves left-back for the last twelve years or so. "See you tomorrow, Fred," he said through the mirror as he combed his hair.

"Er ..... yes, see you Derek," I lied and I was off.

Struggling again.

I was really at a low ebb now, I had officially been written off by a respectable club; if I had been a horse they probably would have shot me!

It was Friday evening at Clough Top Road. Judith had come for tea and we then settled down to a night's television. I was wondering which game to go to watch the next day, I had now been reduced to watching, when there was a knock on the front door, I remember I was sucking an orange as I opened the door.

"The Manager of Crewe Alexandra has asked me to see if you can play for them tomorrow." It was Paul Doherty, now head of sport for Granada Television, standing there. "They are desperately short of players," he went on. "They must be," I thought, "to want a cripple to play for them," but I agreed to play the next day at Gresty Road against Scunthorpe United.

I bandaged my leg up so much I looked like 'The Mummy' as I trotted down the tunnel wondering if it would stand up to the next 90 minutes.

We drew 1-1; I scored the goal and as I was about to leave and thank them for the game I was offered a contract. Only a short three-month one, but I felt in my circumstances it was quite fair of them. So I changed at Crewe hoping for a change of fortune.

I was able to travel each day by train and my travelling companions taught me a lot and helped me regain my confidence, which had taken a battering in the last couple of seasons. Billy Haydock, Peter Leigh, Norman Bodell and Dave Whelan were all hardened pros of varying personalities and temperaments and I learnt more about life, travelling for three months with them, than in the rest of my life until then.

Peter Leigh was an ex-City player who went on to play a record number of games for Crewe. He was a thoroughly nice person and I respected him a great deal. He had his own window cleaning round in the afternoons thinking ahead to the days when he would quit football.

Billy Haydock, also an ex-City player whom I knew from my days at Maine Road, possessed a razor-sharp wit and an ability to find a person's Achilles heel and play on it unmercifully. As the youngest member I was an obvious target, and sometimes he was merciless on me, but I didn't mind and it definitely helped me to cope.

Dave Whelan was a full-back who had tragically broken his leg in the 1960 Cup Final playing for Blackburn Rovers. I was at the game, and since he had been transferred to Crewe he had bought himself a little shop with his savings.

Shrewd bloke, I thought; it was exactly what I intended to do. As the years rolled by, his shops became an Empire of Supermarkets and he eventually sold out his chain of stores, which left him a millionaire. I didn't see him again until many years later when I pulled up next to him in his Rolls Royce at the traffic lights, and waved to him and he waved back like 'The Duke of Edinburgh', but I didn't feel too bad as I purred away in my own brand-new Rolls.

Not bad for a couple of scrubbers from Crewe!

Finally there was Norman Bodell, who although older than me was my special pal.

He took me under his wing and really looked after me.

Norman was a handsome bachelor who seemed to come to the station from a different direction every morning with eyes like 'spit holes in the snow' and used to stroll through training. He became coach of Birmingham City, one of the best in the country, and he made sure players didn't train the way he used to.

These then were Crewe's best players and my travelling companions and although Crewe at the time were on the crest of a slump I still found it difficult to break into the team, but thankfully my leg was standing up to the strain and was never to trouble me again. I could kick a ball beautifully now, accurately long distance or short, which was really good news because I couldn't do that before I was injured!

It was whilst I was at Gresty Road that I began to see the

light; within twelve months I had gone from a First Division club to two Fourth Division clubs and I could just picture myself drifting around the teams in the lower divisions until the day came for me to hang up my boots with nothing to my name and no career to fall back on. Maybe I was becoming more mature and responsible because I found the prospect quite frightening.

After one particularly bad result we were told to report back for extra training in the afternoon and I arrived back in Manchester at the unearthly hour of four-thirty in the afternoon!

As the train pulled in, Norman rushed me along the platform. "Come on, let's hurry up before we get caught up with the ants." This was his rather unflattering description of normal, everyday, hardworking people who were all rushing from work for their tea.

"Yes, let's get away before all those workers," I replied.

Only a matter of weeks later I was desperately trying to become 'an ant' myself and finding that it wasn't such an easy club to join ..... surely I don't have to have a trial for that too.

My short contract was due to end the next day. My leg felt great and I'd scored a lot of goals for the reserves, when the Manager, Jim McGuigan, called the entire playing staff into the boardroom and announced that as from that day he was the new Manager of Grimsby Town.

Great! one day to go on my contract and no Manager to offer me a new one. The reserve team manager, Ernie Tagg, the local milkman, was put in charge of the club and as he didn't know whether he would be Manager for a day or a year, couldn't or wouldn't, whichever it may have been, offer me a new one.

As far as I was concerned that was definitely it ..... I'd had enough sickeners to last me a lifetime, I would now sign for a non-league club and sort out my future life with a steady job .... but that was not as easy as it sounds.

twenty

A HARD JOB
GETTING A JOB

Sorting out the football side of my proposed new life was not too difficult.

When you are just coming from a Football League club there are no shortages of offers, and my advice to any player making this move is to make sure you get the best wage you can because every move you make after that, the money drops a little bit.

I was quite impressed by Buxton Football Club; the Chairman was a very nice chap, Mr Wheatcroft, who used to sit at the next table to me and the City lads whilst we had our lunch at the UCP on Oxford Street. He always said "Anytime you decide to go part-time make sure you let us know before anyone else."

So at the age of 20 I turned my back on professional football on a full-time basis and signed for Buxton, who were managed by ex-Sheffield Wednesday full-back Norman Curtis.

He played full-back as well as managed the club and I had the thankless job of playing in front of him and doing his running, because he must have been about 40 even then!

The ground up in the hills was well kept and I was looking forward to playing non-league football.

This class of football is something different from league football; obviously the rules of the game are the same on the field, but in those days very little else was, and it was here that my soccer education really began.

It is of a much higher standard than people think, less finesse maybe, but much more physical and competitive than the football league. Many is the seasoned pro who has dropped into non-league football expecting a cushy number only to recieve a rude awakening because while he was trying clever tricks on the ball he was dumped unceremoniously onto the seat of his pants by a burly defender who cared nothing for past reputations.

I was not a hard physical player, preferring to rely on skill, but I soon learnt to look after myself; I had to or get crushed, in fact I came off after one game with a bruised and lacerated leg in need of a few stitches ...... but couldn't find out who it belonged to!

One of the coaches who helped to toughen me up was Alan Ball Senior when I played for him at Oswestry Town. He used to bring his famous son to some of the local games and after one game at New Brighton I was driving home when my car broke down in the Mersey Tunnel. Alan and his son were in the car behind me and wanted to tow me out, but I refused ..... I didn't want people saying I'd been dragged out of the Mersey Tunnel by the Balls .....!

Another feature of non-league football is the quick turnover of players, and in the next few years I was to prove a prime example of this as I sampled the delights of another sixteen clubs (more than Jack Nicklaus!) until I finally hung up my boots fifteen years later. Some were good, some not so good, some downright diabolical, but each one of them invaluable to my experience because in all I played under 29 Managers and an incredible 82 coaches who supervised me for over 1,000 games plus 43 games in eighteen countries around the world including Jamaica, Haiti, Barbados, Trinidad, Canada, United States, and I was also a member of the only British team to have played in Cuba. But at the moment I was prepared to give my best for Buxton in the Cheshire League, phase one of the new life of Fred Eyre. Phase two should be no problem because there was a whole world out there waiting to give me a job.

"I'm going to get a job in the morning," I stated quite matter of factly to my Dad this Sunday evening as we settled down with full stomachs to listen to 'Sing Something Simple' on the radio after our Sunday tea; the ham had been first class this week!

"Oh really, what as?" enquired my Dad ..... quite a reasonable question to ask. "Anything really, I'll get a few and pick the best," I replied.

I set off for town in my Morris 1000. It was a beautiful black car JEN 269, funny how you always remember the number plate of your first car.

I was to meet Bob and Paul Aimson and Derek Panter, who were to be my advisers on which of the offers I was sure to receive would suit my talents best.

We decided to attack the big firms first.

"May we see your personnel Manager, please," Bob demanded as a dragon appeared from behind a partition to answer the little brass bell that each of us couldn't resist the urge to clang.

"One ring would have sufficed," she said airily. "Do you all want a job?" "No," replied Bob, my spokesman for the occasion. "Just Mr Eyre here," pointing to me as I straightened my tie in readiness to accept the offer.

"What do you do?" she asked.

"Er ..... anything," I replied.

"Well what have you been doing up to now?"

"A footballer," I said proudly. "We don't need any of them," she said sarcastically. "What qualifications have you got?" she went on.

"He takes a great corner," Derek volunteered.

"And he's very good on free kicks," added Paul.

"I mean academically, how many GCE's or City and Guilds, anything, milk bottle tops, Weetabix cards, anything at all?"

I shook my head. "You've no chance of getting a job here," she said, "or anywhere else by the sound of it. I should try the building sites."

"Don't be put off by that old bag," Bob reassured me, as we proceeded to knock on the door of at least a dozen more com-

panies around town with the same result and same advice .....
try a building site.

Eventually after about six days of this and being refused by
approximately 30 firms in this time it began to dawn on me that
I simply didn't have anything to offer.

I tried the biscuit works in Crumpsall, now immortalised by
Mike Harding, whose early life was spent overlooking them.
My Mother, when money was a bit tight, worked there, four
evenings a week for 28 bob. I was hoping to get more than that,
but I didn't even have the qualifications to pick biscuits off a
conveyor belt and was turned down; they must be crackers!

We were now trying the outlying areas of Manchester and
still getting knock backs; my pals, this is when you know what
real pals are, were getting as dispirited as me.

Days turned into weeks and still nothing. Eventually we did
as everybody had suggested and went to a building site, and I
presented myself, all ten stone four of me (wringing wet) to
the foreman's office.

"Plenty of jobs available here as a hod carrier," he said.
"Do you think you are up to the work," he continued eyeing my
frame doubtfully.

"Yes, I think so," I said, "give me a trial run if you like, I'll
just go and hang my coat in that hut over there."

"That's not a hut ..... it's your hod," he said.

Phew! Even though I was desperate there was no chance that
I could do that.

I tried the cigarette factory where my Auntie Sylvia and
Uncle Arthur worked.

Nothing ..... what a drag!

I tried a plumber's merchants, again nothing doing .....
keep plugging away! A big bakery in Trafford Park was next.
"We'll put you on our waiting list" ..... a small crumb of
comfort.

Maybe 'Washy' would give me another chance in the parks.
No! things were not quite that bad yet ..... bad, but not that
bad.

I thought I'd cracked it the next day as the lads pushed me

into the wallpaper factory in Blackley Village and I asked to see whoever was in charge.

He strode out of his office and before I had chance to say anything he said:

"Aren't you Fred Eyre?"

"Yes," I said.

"Ex-Manchester City?"

"Yes."

"Used to go to Ducie Avenue with Bob Smith didn't you?"

"Yes, he's downstairs," I said warming to the man.

I brought Bob up to join in this heartening conversation.

"Did you know Mark Sidebottom at Ducie?" he went on.

"Course we do ..... old Sidearse is a great pal of ours," we chorused. His face changed to a scowl as he rapped back at us "Well, I'm his Father, Mr Sidearse ..... and there are no vacancies here."

Back to the streets. I was really struggling, my parents were obviously keeping me at home but I felt I was contributing nothing towards my upkeep and also I was relying on my Buxton wages to live on because I absolutely refused to go on the dole.

It was one thing that I really got annoyed about. People who thought they were trying to help me by suggesting I go down to the Labour Exchange, Aytoun Street, were really taken aback when I turned on them very angrily and unfairly and told them what I thought of their suggestion.

"The day will never dawn when Fred Eyre goes on the dole," I remember telling one unfortunate individual, but I must admit I was wobbling a bit.

I almost succumbed one day though, when I was on my own and didn't have the support of my loyal pals.

I went down to Aytoun Street, opened the door of the Labour Exchange—the smell of stale cigarettes nearly knocked my head off.

I felt like a spot on a domino in there. I think I was the only English man in sight, as people of every colour and creed queued up to be spoken to by a man behind a grille.

I walked in about three yards, surveyed the scene, took one look at the imbecile behind the counter who was sorting the jobs out for these out of work people, and thought "He's got a job and I haven't". I stared at him in his moth-eaten suit, with his unshaven face, his frayed cuffs and dirty collar on his shirt, glanced at my reflection in the glass door, immaculate, in my best suit, beautiful clean white shirt and tie, razor creased trousers and spotless shining shoes, turned on my heel and left. I was on the premises for about a minute and a half. "I'll never set foot in there again," I vowed.

There's got to be something for me out there somewhere.

In the evenings Bob and I decided to take 'The FA Coaching Course' under the guidance of Harold Hassall, former Bolton Wanderers and England inside forward who had played in the famous 'Matthews Cup Final' of 1953 when after being 3-1 down in the second half Blackpool pulled back to win 4-3 with Stanley Matthews at long last winning a Cup Final Medal.

Harold Hassall was now an FA Coach and even though it was early days, I felt instinctively at home in a track suit, confident in front of a group of boys, and conversant with the subject that I was being taught, how to teach people to play football, I hadn't succeeded to a great degree myself, but it didn't mean I couldn't teach other people how to do it and thoroughly enjoyed the course and was not in the least surprised when I passed my badge with ease, at the age of twenty.

This meant I could now go out into the world and be paid for coaching groups, teams, or anybody who wanted me to teach them.

Looking back it was an impressive squad of would-be coaches who attended this course every week.

My pal Bob went on to become Manager of Bury, Port Vale and Swindon Town and a very successful one too; at one time he was the youngest Manager in the Football League.

Wilf Tranter from Manchester United became Bob's assistant at Swindon.

Billy Urmson is now coach at Oldham Athletic, Eammon Dunphy went on to represent his country, Eire, many times in

[Left] Crosslee 22nd May 1951, 4th from right, middle row. Next left Malcolm Roberts.

[Below] 30 Clough Top Road. The pavement in front of the house doubled as Wembley Stadium in the winter and Lords in the summer.

[Above] The seeds are sown, my first ever game and a great view of 'Swifty'.

I seem to have been playing with 'donkeys' all my life!

The only way to learn the game ..... playing in the street with a small ball and with lads nine or ten years older than yourself.

My Dad in his 'prime'.

Not really a stroke for the purists, but we didn't care in Boggart Hole Clough. My pal Mike Roddy in action with the bat ..... is that Godfrey Evans behind the stumps!

I'd waited hours to see this ..... Roy Paul with the cup, Dave Ewing, Don Revie, Bill Leivers and Roy Clarke ..... can't wait for it to be my turn.

Butlins July 3rd 1963 ..... a board meeting was held to decide whether Lincoln City was to be the lucky club to obtain my signature. The vote seems unanimous!

"This is Ted Eyre!" I am introduced to Bill Anderson and trainer Bill McGlen, together with the other new signings from the left Terry Thorne, Alan Spears and Alan Morton.

Ducie Avenue, a great team. I'm seated first left on the front row. In later years when Bob Smith became a famous Manager he could afford a pair of laces for his boots! Front row second from right.

When I was full of hope.

Manchester City Football Club 1960.

Boots by courtesy of Colin Barlow, pads by courtesy of the Manchester Evening News and a stomach full of Mars Bars. All the north's top young stars will be on view!

'Lapping'-up the training. Fourth pair from the front with my partner John Benson, now Assistant Manager of Manchester City.

Pre-season training at Lincoln city. A rare picture of me at the front!

The transformation nearly completed. My first shop in Booth Street.

Manager and Skipper before the game at New York Cosmos. With Chris Davies.
Leading out the troops v Canadian National team, Ontario, Canada.

The End! My last game in Trinidad, my face shows I'm ready for retiring.

Manager and Assistant for a day, me with Dave Brooks on the day of our appointment.

This is a shirt! A welcome to Springfield Park for Larry Lloyd.

the future and is now coaching back in his native country, and I am now coach at Wigan Athletic, so I think Harold Hassall can congratulate himself on a job well done.

I know I left the course with a feeling that I had something to offer in this direction, but my main priority at the moment was to find some form of employment.

I was meeting Bob again this day for my daily onslaught of unsuspecting companies. I had tried every single day, hardly any escaped my attention; at this rate I would soon have exhausted them all.

As I was going to meet him I met my former City colleague Peter Dobing in Albert Square. Peter was an expensive signing for City from Blackburn Rovers, a fabulous inside forward who eventually moved to Stoke City to continue his career.

"How's things?" he said.

"Not bad. I'm going to start looking for a job next week," I told him, in my mind thinking of all the refusals I'd had.

"You'll have no problem," he said as he waved cheerio.

"If only you knew," I thought as I hurried to meet Bob.

I needed to buy a birthday card that day, so I suggested that I do this first before the chore of job hunting.

We could have chosen anywhere to make my purchase, but Alan Wardle, a full-back at Manchester United, worked part-time in a stationer's shop in the afternoons so I thought I might as well patronise his establishment and have a chat with him at the same time.

So we cut through to St Peter's Square and into Caldwell's; the card department was on the first floor.

Unknown to me the shop was owned by a Manchester City Supporter, Mr Chris Muir, who was eventually to become a director of the club.

I was selecting my card as he strolled over to say "Hello!"

We had a brief chat about City and I inquired if Alan was in.

"Och! he left two weeks ago," he informed me in his rich Scottish accent.

Bob immediately rolled his eyes and nodded towards Mr Muir from behind his back. I didn't really need Bob's silent hint. ''Er, have you got anybody to take his place, only I'm looking for a job,'' I said as Bob retreated into the distance to leave me to it.

Mr Muir looked me up and down and simply said ''OK, if you don't like it after six months you can leave and if I don't like you after six months you can still leave''.

I couldn't ask for anything straighter or fairer than that, so on the following Monday morning I reported to Caldwell's Stationers in St Peter's Square to become an ant.

twenty-one

A CRASH COURSE IN NON-LEAGUE FOOTBALL

I had never done a day's work in my life before. I didn't know an invoice from a delivery note, but I had a couple of things going for me. I was grateful for the opportunity, and as with my football, I was willing to work hard and give it everything I had.

I also had the added bonus of having a tremendous respect and admiration for the Boss, Mr Muir, and I had no intention of letting him down.

Mr Muir is a proud Scotsman, very keen on football and knowledgeable too about the game, not really one of the main qualifications of a football club Director, and on the business side I was impressed by his capacity for hard work.

If a floor needed sweeping, he would sweep it. If some heavy furniture required humping, his would be the first jacket off and he was getting stuck in while everybody else was still thinking about it; he also possessed a shrewd and quick-thinking business brain and I loved to watch him in action.

His motto was "The customer is **nearly** always right". He would bend over backwards to be of service but if ever a customer went that bit too far and began to take liberties .....
chop! he would tell them exactly what he thought, fair and straight to the point. Just the man for me to have as my Boss.

I have carried this motto on as I moved into business on my own.

Weights of paper, sizes of paper, sizes of envelopes, rulings of books; when somebody asked for the A4 I told him I thought it ran from Bristol to London!

But I really relished the challenge and set about learning from the word go. I loved serving in the shop, dealing with people.

There is something about a stationer's shop which brings out the best in people, so many different things, little novelties. People just come in and have a rummage round and always find something they need.

Caldwell's was one of the best, in fact, I thought it was **the** best, and I was learning every day. My mates would come in for a chat and be amazed that I could serve people confidently and correctly with all these strange things and also give correct change as well.

I had the occasional pang of course, like the morning Mike Doyle bobbed in to see me and told me he was making his league debut at Cardiff that evening; the whippersnapper was on his way to a great career. Good luck to him, he was a fine young player and was in my team that fateful day when I did my leg in against Bury, but that was now definitely a thing of the past. "Good luck tonight, Mike," I said sincerely as he left the shop with left back Vic Gommersall, another old pal, and I returned to my Bics and envelopes.

"Your six months are up," began Mr Muir as I walked in to see him at his request, "have you enjoyed it here?" "I have, actually, much more than I thought I might," I replied. "Well! I would like to make you the Manager of the place from now on, what do you think?"

I thought briefly of the other people employed at the shop who had been there much longer than me, but without hesitation accepted my promotion gratefully.

I was to succeed Arthur Gee, another person who was a big help to me when I first started, who was moving to become Boss of a London-based stationers who were opening in Manchester. I had buckled down to the job, tried my best, and at last was getting some reward.

On the football side signing for Buxton was becoming less

of a good idea as each week went by. The trips over the Pennines were a hazardous task and two car crashes within six weeks convinced me that a club in a less precarious part of the North would be a much safer bet for me.

The week previously the car carrying a couple of my team mates had hit a sheep and killed it as I followed in the car behind, and this particular evening I was travelling alone. The weather was appalling and really I had a heaven sent excuse for not turning up at training that night, but I had never missed a session and I thought it would be OK.

Training in the evenings was one of the things I found difficult to get used to at first, having spent all my football life training in the mornings, but I was acclimatised to it now and it was fairly enjoyable.

The roads were becoming more and more treacherous as I came over the tops and could see the lights of Buxton twinkling below me, only about three miles to go.

I slowly came down the hill and turned the wheel to negotiate a right-hand bend at the bottom, but as I turned the wheel the car simply continued to go straight.

The wall, made up of large boulders, came looming towards me as I wrestled with the wheel. I careered through the wall, a huge boulder crashing through the windscreen and coming to rest next to me on the front passenger seat.

As the car rolled over, the boulder and I bounced about inside the car together, like the last two Smarties left in the tube. The car finished up back on its wheels again at the foot of the ditch, and I ended up back in the driver's seat with the boulder occupying the passenger seat.

I scrambled out, left the boulder to fend for itself, clambered back up the hill and got to the top just in time for a huge lorry to take exactly the same route as I had and bounce down the same ditch, coming to rest about two inches away alongside my little car, where I had been standing not half a minute earlier.

That was the end of JEN 269. Six weeks later another crash, and that was the end of my trips to Buxton, because I received

an offer to join New Brighton ..... a big mistake, but you don't
know these things at the time as I began my long and varied
trek around the more sordid areas of football.

New Brighton was a former league club which years earlier
had been forced to apply for re-election; this is usually a
formality but this particular year they had been unlucky and
they were voted out.

The stadium was a fine one, but 'The Rakers' had obviously
found life tough in non-league and had obviously seen better
days.

From the town centre of Manchester, through the busy
streets of Salford, down the East Lancs Road, through to the
heart of Liverpool, through the Mersey Tunnel and another
half an hour from there through Wallasey to the ground was
not a journey to relish; in fact it was impossible to even contemplate. It took in those days at the heart of the rush hour approximately two hours.

I didn't mind doing it on match days, but every Tuesday
evening and every Thursday evening as well was out of the
question, which was what I told the Manager when he first
approached me.

"Don't worry, sign for us, just travel through on match days
and train anywhere you like during the week."

I arranged to train at Ashton United with their players, and
Hyde United as a second choice. Both clubs were very helpful
so I duly signed on the dotted line on a Wednesday night and
played for New Brighton the following Saturday—we lost
1-2 to Wigan Athletic.

"See you Tuesday," the Manager said to me after the
match. "Oh! a midweek game," I thought.

"Yes, OK, who are we playing?" I replied.

"No game ..... training!"

"Don't forget I've arranged to train in Manchester," I
reminded him.

"It doesn't state that in your contract," he said sounding
more like a solicitor than the painter and decorator he was.

I realised I had made a mistake by not getting my special

clause written into my contract, so now I didn't have a leg to stand on and although I hadn't been there five minutes, I knew I wasn't in for a long association with this club.

I kept it going until Christmas, when I just had to leave. I was spending all my life in my car, and even though I didn't have a club to go to I simply asked for and got my release ..... another lesson learned the hard way; good job petrol was only about half a crown a gallon in those days.

I had brief spells at a couple more local Cheshire league clubs where I served under a variety of coaches. One night one of them had us lined up in front of the stand, shaking hands and bowing our heads slightly as he walked along regally in front of us and graciously shook each player's hand.

"What on earth are you doing?" inquired the Manager, who had come out to inspect the session.

"I'm showing the lads what to do when they meet the King at Wembley."

"Don't you mean the Queen?" said the Manager.

"By the time this lot get to Wembley it will be the King again!" said the coach ..... not true but it summed up some of my non-league days nicely, they took the game but didn't take themselves, too seriously.

I also encountered a couple of trainers during this period who were a law unto themselves. Not coaches, but sponge-men, the old-fashioned type where the 'magic sponge' ruled OK. In one game I rose majestically above the centre forward to head a corner away and came crashing down from a great height over his head because he hadn't jumped.

I thought I'd broken my back as I lay prostrate, gasping for breath as our trainer came on. "My back's bad," I gasped as he reached me. "Which one?" he replied. "How many backs do you think I've got?" I said angrily.

"It could be your right back or it could be your left back," he informed me, thumped the sponge in my face and departed.

In another game our right winger took a terrible knock on his ankle and it was visibly swelling before our eyes as we gathered round him before the trainer actually reached him;

it was an enormous size and looked really bad.

His face had gone white and he was actually being sick so severe was the pain, our trainer carefully untied his laces, eased his boot gently off, each movement accompanied by a groan from the poor lad and finally managed to ease his sock off.

"Oh! Arthur," said the trainer with a look of horror on his face, "That's really bad, I can't stand that."

"Tell me the worst, what is it?" groaned Arthur.

"Your feet smell terrible," replied our heartless trainer. He also administered treatment to injuries during the week, if you had a headache he would put your head under the heat lamp. I told him I had sinus trouble and he got me some pills from the doctor, but it made my breathing worse when he pushed them up my nose.

His favourite remedy to injuries was "It's in the mind—run it off". Many an ankle looked black and blue to me but according to him we were only imagining it was bruised.

One day one of my team mates came into the treatment room on crutches while this trainer had gone for a cup of tea. He put his crutches behind the door and hopped across the room and just made it onto the treatment table. A few seconds later the trainer returned, examined the offending leg, which was eventually diagnosed as a hairline fracture, slapped him firmly on the thigh. "Run it off," he commanded. The young lad looked amazed but didn't argue, swung his legs off the bed and promptly collapsed in a heap on the floor. "Christ, I'd better get you to the hospital," said our trainer, "somebody has left a pair of crutches behind the door, that was lucky, borrow these and go and get an X-Ray!"

Whilst playing for Crewe, ironically at Lincoln, our right winger, Andy Haddock, went on one of his jinking runs, but this time he jinked smack into his beefy opponent and when he emerged his nose was spread all over his face and nothing could stop the blood flowing ..... until our resourceful trainer solved the problem by stuffing handfuls of grass up his nostrils. He always liked to get to the root of the problem!

Then Alan Ball took me to Oswestry Town, another long journey, but this time I was becoming more experienced and had the 'training clause' inserted into the contract.

I really looked forward to playing for Alan Ball, he had impressed me enormously whenever he had deputised for Harold Hassall on my coaching course by his sheer profession-alism and knowledge of the game, and it was little wonder that his son Alan had inherited these qualities from his Dad.

Indeed, I remember them both from years ago. Before I'd met him I was marking his son in a match at Bromwich Street in his junior days with Bolton Wanderers. Young Alan was only tiny, but he could look after himself even then and Alan senior was giving him hell from the touchline, but it was all good, constructive stuff and the lad has certainly reaped the benefit.

I was hoping for the same and I needed no persuasion to sign for Alan and looked forward to Saturday's game at Elles-mere Port, because Alan had already told me I would play great because I was a great player ..... he told all his players this.

I should have said to myself "If I'm such a great player what the hell am I doing playing for Oswestry?" but No! if Alan said I was a great player ..... a great player I was.

I travelled direct to Ellesmere Port and met my team-mates for the first time an hour before the kick-off.

They looked an odd sort of bunch. I knew big Jack Abbott from our days together at Crewe, I was introduced to skipper Gerry Broadhead, who said nothing in return but clenched a fist under my nose and said "We get stuck in here." Gerry was 'Mr Oswestry' and my wing half partner (he obviously thought even before I was stripped that I wasn't physical enough for his team) , and "this is 'Curly' Rogers, our left winger," was my final introduction. 'Curly' Rogers—it must be a joke. You only read about that sort of a name in 'The Wizard' or 'The Hotspur' or any other boys' magazine.

"Hiya, Curly," I chirped and he flashed me a friendly grin revealing a set of teeth that looked as though they belonged to somebody else.

Actually he was a nice lad ..... but 'Curly' Rogers—unbelievable. I never found out what his real name was.

With fifteen minutes to go before the kick-off I casually mentioned to Gerry, ''Where's Alan?'' thinking he must make an entrance about five to three to make more of an impact on his players.

''He doesn't come on match days,'' said Gerry quite matter of factly.

I remember my mouth falling slightly open as I gaped in disbelief.

''He's the bloody Manager and he doesn't come on match days.''

I thought I'd heard a few classics in football up until then but this had the potential to beat the lot, as I eagerly followed up my line of questioning.

''How does he pick the team then?''

''I tell him whose played well,'' replied Gerry, who was now taking more of a prominent position in my thoughts. ''And who tells him how you have played?'' I went on. ''It doesn't matter, he always plays,'' chipped in one of the other lads. I didn't like what I was hearing one little bit and finally the $64,000 question.

''Why is he not here on match days?''

''Because he's also Manager of Nantwich Town and he can't be in two places at once.''

I slumped back on my seat. We were due on the field any minute and I was trying to take it all in. I had signed for a club whose Manager didn't watch us play, the Captain was an automatic choice, and if you got on the wrong side of him you probably would be out of the side, plus we had 'Curly' Rogers on the left wing! We only needed 'Roy of the Rovers' at centre forward and we would have the lot.

I had never heard of anything like Alan's position with two clubs before or since, until his son went one better and seemed to be a player at Southampton, a player at Vancouver Whitecaps and Manager of Blackpool. Young Alan's son is going to have to go a bit to beat that in the future if he wants to keep the family record going.

I was pleasantly surprised by our display though and we beat the much stronger Ellesmere Port team one nil. Gerry Broadhead scored the goal, he would be able to give himself a good report.

I wasn't too happy with the closed-shop attitude I detected there between a couple of the regular local players—they seemed to just play for themselves—and during one game when they were obviously all messing about together, I let them know at the end of the game what I thought of their selfish performances.

As I got into the bath, my mate Jim McKiernan, a goal-scoring centre forward said:

"That's you out for the next game," and he was right too.

After the game I rang Alan Ball, who had again not been there, and inquired if I was out for good. He didn't even know I had missed that game and immediately restored me to the team for the next game and for the remainder of the season.

Eventually Alan did harness his full attention to one job and quit Nantwich to come to us, and I thoroughly enjoyed playing for him, and secretly I was hoping that my chance for a return to league football had not gone, as the scouts flocked to see us. But goalkeeper Stuart Sherratt was the main target and eventually this fine keeper signed for Port Vale and I kept plugging away, but under Alan, I felt I had improved a bit more and my confidence was high.

twenty-two
A HONEYMOON
IN SHREWSBURY

On the business side I was really happy with my progress. Mr Muir was becoming more and more involved in his attempt to become a director of Manchester City, but the old board of directors was holding firm against mounting pressures from Press and public alike to stand down and let the younger vigorous 'Ginger Group' of which Mr Muir was a key figure, take over and help to regain some of the past glories for the club.

In addition to this he was pursuing his ambition of becoming a member of Parliament by standing for election in one of Manchester's local elections, so all of these activities meant he was spending more and more time away from the business.

This meant increased responsibility for me. He had also taken possession of the little shop in Booth Street from where I'd bought my scrapbook and this needed looking after. A shop on Liverpool Road in Salford and one in Stretford completed the set.

I really relished the extra responsibility and dabbled in every aspect of the business, as well as serving in the shop. I helped with the buying, the accounts, correspondence to customers and suppliers alike; I chased up overdue orders, attended to our many commercial accounts, sold office furniture and typewriters, absolutely everything, sorted out any minor staff problem and generally enjoyed working for a living.

I was extremely happy at Caldwell's, the staff were friendly and always there was Mr Muir setting a fine example at the top.

This new found stability and worry-free existence prompted me to think that maybe Judith, who had stood by me through all my troubles, might care to join me in the matrimonial stakes.

With her wages from TAP (Portuguese Airlines) and mine from Caldwell's plus my football money, I reckoned we could manage safely and so on 21st May 1966 we were married at St. Chrysostoms Church, Victoria Park.

I was up bright and early, my best man, ex-City team mate Derek Panter, and I looking our best as we made our way to the Church.

Unknown to me while we were both actually standing at the altar, Judith was still in bed! Her nerves had got the better of her and she was feeling too ill to stand, let alone walk down the aisle.

In the end a few sharp words and threats from my new brother-in-law-to-be, Mr Dixon, got her onto her feet and she finally arrived, just as Derek was saying "I think she's changed her mind!" much to the relief of the organist, whose fingers by this time were wearing out. It's a pity Ric didn't still own 'The Oasis', maybe now as a member of the family I could have strolled behind the counter and poured myself a cup of coffee! But he had moved up in the world of show business by this time.

Our honeymoon was to be in London, but after one day we had to travel to Shrewsbury where Oswestry were playing Shrewsbury Town in a Cup Final at the picturesque 'Gay Meadow' ground.

I received the usual ribald comments from the lads as I arrived at the ground, bits of confetti still falling occasionally out of my clothes as I prepared to take part in the most bizarre game I have ever played in.

I was marking Peter Broadbent, the ex-England and Wolverhampton Wanderers player, who had been a great player in his time and a vital player in the great Wolves team of the 'fifties. Now he was nearing the end of his career but I was still looking forward to pitting my wits against him.

With one minute to go the score was an amazing 4-4; the little non-league side had played its heart out to really stagger our third division opponents. The ball was punted out of our defence to Jim McKiernan who was on the right wing, loitering without intent! He set off down the line and I decided to take a deep breath and make one last-gasp effort to pull out the winner. While Jim was progressing down the wing past a maze of weary defenders, I was galloping down the middle as he slung over a very high cross to about the penalty spot; it was really too near the keeper but I kept running ..... just in case. For some reason keeper Alan Boswell, an experienced campaigner, completely misjudged the cross and I ran in behind him and gleefully headed the ball into the net, before turning joyfully to run the length of the stand jumping and doing cartwheels as my team mates jubilantly hung round my neck.

Suddenly there wasn't any cheering and we all turned to see what the problem was, just in time to see a mass of blue shirts converging on our goal like the 'Charge of the Light Brigade.' The referee had astonishingly given me offside, even though I must have run 90 yards from behind the ball and now poor old Charlie Hughes was picking the ball out of our net and we had lost 4-5!

What a honeymoon, does nothing ever go right in football!

It was a silent honeymoon drive back home to our new semi-detached we had bought ourselves in Radcliffe, an industrial suburb between Bury and Manchester, to start our married life.

I had hoped to begin our life together with a goal at Shrewsbury but as I thought more about it I had a bigger goal in life to aim for ..... I wanted a business of my own like Mr Muir's.

twenty-three

A "KOSHER" COACH

During the summer my best man, Derek Panter, moved from City via Torquay United to Ellesmere Port, and after he had signed, the Manager, Cyril Tolley said to him:

"All I need now is a really good wing half to complete my team, do you know one?" Derek being the good mate he is said: "No! ..... but I know Fred Eyre!"

So at his request I went to see Mr Tolley, a big, brusque schoolteacher who offered to treble my wages if I signed for Ellesmere Port. Just married, wages trebled, I didn't hesitate and so I became an Ellesmere Port player. Not bad, five non-league clubs in two seasons! ..... but there were still plenty more to go at.

Ellesmere Port had decided that this would be their big season, they would really 'push the boat out' regarding wages and recruit the best players available by offering attractive wages and lucrative bonuses.

I felt it was a good side and we played well at the beginning of the season, winning most of our games.

Unfortunately we were knocked out of the FA Cup in the first preliminary round and whilst all the players felt very disappointed that we wouldn't be playing Arsenal or somebody like that at Wembley the following May, we didn't think it was the end of the world and immediately after the game we were all giving the usual excuse when anybody has lost a cup game "We'll be able to concentrate on the league now."

Unfortunately the committee members were far from pleased and had other ideas.

Committee members are a breed of their own, and I have experienced one or two who are from the top drawer.

One was so lifeless it is rumoured he had been dead for a week but nobody had told him!

We used to say he read the morning paper in bed each morning and always turned to the obituary column first, if his name wasn't in it, he would then get up!

Committee members, even though they never actually have the nerve to say anything to the players, always manage to make their feelings known in the social club or anywhere else the spectators gather to have a drink and a moan, and usually it was from a supporter one would learn of any impending transfer or topic happening within the club.

This usually was the case at badly run clubs. The good clubs with strong Managers invariably did things a little more professionally.

Unfortunately for me, most of my non-league career was spent in the first section with a host of 'trainee corpses' at the helm.

Before one game at Fleetwood the club took us to Madame Tussauds in Blackpool as a form of relaxation before the game and they asked the Chairman of the committee to keep moving because they were stock-taking!

After the latest cup defeat the committee members were at their best, clucking around like old hens and totally ignoring the players after the game, who although we had done our best had committed the unforgivable crime of losing.

After much tutting and whispering we were all gathered together and informed by the Manager (there was not a committee member in sight at the time) that our wages from that moment were to be cut by 75% and would we all be kind enough to raise our hands as acceptance of this 'fait accompli'.

My first reaction to this outrage was one of mild amusement. Imagine the reception of the committee if we had won the cup-

tie and had asked them for a 75% **increase** in our wages .....
"No chance" would have been the unanimous answer to the
reduction.

Therefore I was astonished to see ten hands being raised,
mine being the only one to hang limply from my shoulder.
I must be dreaming, I thought, as the Manager thanked the
players for the 'unanimous gesture'.

As the players all shuffled from the room, mumbling and
muttering—we can all mumble and mutter in disgust but not
one of them had said a single word in defence of the situation—
I made my way over to the Manager and informed him that he
had conveniently overlooked the fact that I personally had not
raised my hand in acceptance of the drastic wage cut and
therefore was expecting to be paid in full at the week-end
as it stated in my contract.

He looked at me as though I had 'Judas' printed on my
tracksuit not 'Adidas' and informed me I would be getting the
reduced wage the same as everybody else.

This act by the club was totally against my principles.
I took my case to the 'Football Association' and although as I
expected I won it conclusively it was obvious I would be on the
move again.

Two more local moves provided more experience but not a
lot of pleasure. At Radcliffe Borough, round the corner from
our new home, we always trained in the dark. Manager Ray
Gill, who still holds the record for league appearances for
Chester, used to work wonders at varying our training but was
obviously limited in the dark—we did our sprints on the pavement of the main thoroughfare under the light of a lamp post!

One night's training consisted of erecting a huge fence
behind the goal, to stop the ball going into the big reservoir
everytime a shot at goal was off target during a game—my fitness didn't improve but I now knew how to knock posts into the
ground!

Eventually I arrived at Chorley and for the first time since
my Buxton days I felt as though I had joined a club of some
substance.

The facilities were good, the ground excellent and I felt at home the minute I drove through the gates.

I was to spend a couple of good seasons at Chorley, mostly a happy time and two significant events in my private life would take place whilst I was at Chorley; all in all I was entering an interesting period of my life.

The moment that destined me to sign for Chorley came when I was playing for St Helen's Town; my old mate from Oswestry, Jim McKiernan, had taken over as Manager and asked me to sign.

I enjoyed playing for Jim, but he was the only professional thing about the club. During a break in the game against Chorley I was waiting to take a throw-in whilst our goalkeeper was having treatment from our trainer.

To amuse myself I began juggling the ball from foot to foot, I hadn't had many kicks during the game so I was making up for it.

A voice in the crowd jokingly shouted to me "Keep that up and you will be good enough to sign for Chorley".

I responded to the joke by telling him I wouldn't mind because it looked such a good set up.

The following week I became a Chorley player because the face in the crowd was the Chorley secretary, Jim Moscrop.

As usual I was under the charge of a clueless Manager who preached Liverpool at us the whole time. "Emlyn always takes up a position here, then he knocks it wide to Steve Heighway, who takes on and beats five defenders. I want you to do the same, take on and beat five defenders and then get a good cross in," he would tell our young left winger, who a fortnight previously was playing for 'The Dog and Duck' or some other pub in the local Sunday league.

It was absolutely ludicrous and I was relieved when he was sacked shortly afterwards, but not before he called local lad Ronnie Pickering to one side half an hour before the kick-off to give him his debut.

"Have you ever played in mid-field son?" he said to Ron, who nodded enthusiastically. "Well put number 10 on and play right back!'' Coach Harry McNally and Stan Hayhurst then took over and restored some form of stability to the place. Stan, former Tottenham Hotspur goalkeeper, was the Manager, a gentleman, quiet and respected, whilst Harry, the extrovert, put us through our paces.

I enjoyed Harry's training immensely. It was well thought out, plenty of ball work and Harry's ideas coincided with mine and I was really enjoying my game.

I had also been offered a little coaching job in Manchester every Monday evening, coaching the top Manchester Jewish Football team, Waterpark.

Not exactly starting at the top but for me I couldn't have begun my coaching career at a better place. Jewish boys, many of whom, even at this early age, ran their own successful businesses, employing many people, are not used to anyone telling them what to do.

Even though they took their football seriously, being put through their paces, punished for sloppy training, and being constantly pushed and bullied did not come naturally to them.

They all had minds of their own, were all used to getting their own way and a group of 20 or more of them under one roof was a pretty formidable gathering. But they didn't intimidate me and I ripped into them from the word go and gave them thoroughly professional training and coaching whether they liked it or not. Any slackers were publicly punished with press-ups whilst their friends and colleagues counted them out.

In return, they gave me their utmost respect, did everything I asked of them and more and their efforts and improvement in their play and general standard of fitness gave me a belief in my own ability to coach and the confidence that if I could handle these lads I could handle anybody.

I coached and trained the team for three years and thoroughly enjoyed every minute of it and confirmed my idea that when the day came for me to hang up my boots I had the necessary qualifications to consider being a coach.

My private life continued to prosper and I was now confident that I could handle any aspect of the stationery business and

I knew Mr Muir was pleased with me, but still I hankered after a business of my own and thought it about time I did something about it.

twenty-four

RAINDROPS ARE FALLING ON MY HEAD

Business was a little quiet this particular day. Mr Muir was out, so I decided to have a good look at the stock and try to calculate how much I would need to start a business of my own.

I decided to do my 'stock-take' systematically by starting at the door, working my way through the shop and then into the stockrooms.

Behind the door was a very insignificant stand that housed the various typewriter ribbons. Customers never even saw it as they entered the shop, but when we were asked for a ribbon we just took one from this dispenser stand. I began my stock-take there. Fifteen seconds later my stock-check was over, I had already passed the figure I had in the bank and I hadn't even completed the count of the typewriter ribbons. Absolutely no chance of my getting a shop; I estimated Mr Muir's stock at about £20,000 and I had £150 in the bank.

I was disheartened, but not knocked out, because even though I couldn't see it, I just instinctively knew that there was some way out of this problem, some method of trading, a different approach to the job. I just couldn't figure it out, but I knew it was there, and I chewed the problem over almost every waking hour and often during the night, but couldn't come up with the answer.

It took a downpour to give me a clue as to how I could set up in business by myself, even though I had no money.

A young office girl came into the shop with a list of stationery requirements, she was absolutely soaked to the skin as the rain belted down.

"You should have 'phoned me with your list and I would have delivered the order for you," I volunteered. She was delighted to hear this and promised to do just that in the future.

It occurred to me that there must be other firms who would sooner have their secretaries remain in their offices working, earning their wages by performing more lucrative tasks than the mundane job of traipsing down to the stationer's to pick up their office requirements, especially in the pouring rain.

They could ring me and I would deliver their order to them, they never need leave the confines of their warm, cosy offices and I would be more than happy to get drenched if it meant I was in business on my own.

I needn't carry any stocks, because, I reasoned, as the orders came in I would dash round to the various wholesalers and obtain the goods. So I was only buying stock that was in fact already sold. It all seemed so simple, so I decided to pursue the matter a little further. My investigations into the protocol of the trade revealed that it was frowned upon to work from home, it just wasn't the done thing, and even though I was contemplating starting right at the very bottom, I wanted to do things in the correct manner and not upset anybody. But I needed some form of base, and also somewhere for my prospective customers to ring with their orders.

So every Sunday I walked around the streets of Manchester, back streets, alleys, basements, anything in search of a base, an address from where to start my Empire.

Eventually I decided upon an old women's prison in Lancaster Avenue. It was open plan and had three curving galleries of wood, cast iron and glass. It had been built in 1871 and ran from Fennel Street at one end to Todd Street, near Victoria Station, at the other end, where there was a rather dubious looking night club.

The former cells were now converted into little offices and the cells which looked out onto the main thoroughfare were now little shops, each one a character of its own; a jewellers, antique shop, sign writer, leatherwear shop, greetings cards shop, and it was amongst this odd assortment of traders that I decided to launch Fred Eyre Stationers onto an unsuspecting world.

I took out a lease on number 55, one of the rear view cells on the first landing, for fifteen shillings a week. It measured about 4ft. x 8ft. and was completely bare with no heating, but it was 'home'. I went in to see Mr Muir the next day and handed in my notice. I left Caldwell's on the following Friday and at 8.30 am as I left our home in Radcliffe on the Monday morning 31st July 1967 Fred Eyre Stationers was born ..... no customers, no accounts, no stock, one estate car, an office for 15 bob a week, £150 in the bank, the support of my wife and parents, plenty of optimism and boundless energy. Does anybody need more!

Mr Muir as always was first class, he wished me all the best and said if ever I needed help to go and see him, because a friend in need ..... is a bloody pest!

I was on my own now, and even though I didn't have one single customer, and many that I had dealt with at Caldwells asked me to go and see them when I started, I always refused. I vowed that no matter how much I might struggle I would never, ever, approach any of Mr Muir's customers in an attempt to lure them away to trade with me and I am proud to say I never did; I was prepared to stand or fall by my own efforts.

The lifeline of my new venture was obviously the 'phone. I couldn't be sat by the telephone all day waiting to receive orders if I was out chasing business, so, not for the first time in my life, my dear old Mam came to the rescue. She agreed to stay in all day at home and answer the calls and take the orders. I would ring her from telephone boxes every hour whilst I was on my travels. If we had been lucky and there were one or two orders 'phoned in I would then pick up the necessary stock from the various wholesalers and deliver it pronto to the customer in between my calls to companies whom I was trying to persuade to deal with me.

On my business cards, which I left almost everywhere, was the name and address of my luxurious new premises, but they simply said "For orders ring Cheetham Hill 1200". Nobody bothered to enquire if the 'phone was actually at my Lancaster Avenue premises, they all assumed it was, so I never volunteered the information. They got their orders promptly, so it didn't matter to them that my system was a little unorthodox.

My first call as a self-employed man was to my brother-in-law's business. Perhaps Jill, my wife's sister, would insist that her husband deal with me in order that her sister wouldn't finish in the workhouse! He was now very well known in show business circles with his partners Danny Betesh and Harvey Lisberg and in his usual forthright manner he told me:-

"Yes, you can have our account, but if you let us down even once you will be out of the door, brother-in-law or not." I didn't expect anything else and fifteen years later I am still their 'Stationer to the Stars' doing work for the world's top stars ABBA, Boney M, 10cc, Barry Manilow, Dr Hook, Kate Bush and many many more. If I had let them down I have no doubt he would have been true to his word and booted me out, but I had no intentions of letting him or anyone else down who gave me a chance.

His straightforward approach was one of the reasons why Ric Dixon was so successful in the world of show business and in his own way he tried to help me all he could, thank God I never let him down.

From there I was sent to Ric's accountants to meet John Wright, who gave me the same instructions, "Yes OK, but let me down at your peril". Suits me! A super man to deal with. Then on to George Greenall, who had been a player at City with me, but was now running his own insurance company in Handforth. Same story, another grand lad, then to another ex-City colleague, Geoff Fry, now owner of a fabulous night club in Ashton, all in all a good first day,

The next day though was to be my test, and I was to find out that I was the world's worst salesman.

My calls the previous day were not too difficult because I

knew the four people in question I was going to see, my efforts from this day forward were to be a different story altogether.

I set out to saturate Manchester, leave no office unturned, every single one would be canvassed by me, they would all be bowled over by my charm and personality and be queueing up to give me orders.

I chose a big office block, looked at my watch, thought I won't go in just now they will be on their break, I'll go and have a cup of coffee myself and come back later ..... too near dinner-time, I'll go in after two o'clock, think I'll nip back to Lancaster Avenue and see if the post has brought anything ..... nothing. Back to the office block ..... goodness is that the time already, it's too late in the day to call now they won't want to see me at this time, I'll go in the morning ..... a swift drive home. "Had a good day love, did you get any orders?".

"Hard day love, no orders but I'm really knackered."

I knew I was only fooling myself but I was frightened to death at the prospect of actually knocking on a blank door not knowing the reception I would get. I also knew that if I went on like this we would starve and worse still I would have failed in my venture. I couldn't even contemplate that.

The next morning I set off with good intentions, but as soon as I was confronted by the office door I got an attack of the wobbles. However, this time I would not be deterred and gritted my teeth and knocked on the big imposing oak door, it was opened by a female who looked like Brian London in drag.

"You don't want any stationery, do you?" I said.

"No," she said with a puzzled look on her face.

"Thank you very much," I said as I retreated down the stairs.

Somehow realising I had approached the job in the wrong manner I persisted and was pleased to report at the end of the day that I had been slung out of every office in the building. I was improving, I was at least knocking on the door.

It gave me fresh heart to start the next day. I was now moving up in the world and being ejected from all the most luxurious offices as well as the small firms. It was Thursday and I hadn't earned one single penny when I descended on a travel agency on King Street who at least had the decency to see me.

"So just give me a ring at this number, pointing to my card, "if you need any stationery. It doesn't matter how little and I will deliver it personally within the hour ..... thanks very much, cheerio."

What nice people I thought as I left the premises.

Later in the day I rang in to my Mother's to see if anybody had bothered to contact us with an order. The unbelievable had happened, an order at last, should I spend the profit on steak or chicken for our tea?

"It's from a travel agency on King Street," my Mother informed me, sounding as excited as I was. "I knew they were good people," I thought.

"They want a packet of paper clips" ..... Mother began,

"Yes OK, Mam, I've got that, what else?"

"That's it," she said.

"You mean that's all they want, a packet of paper clips, it can't be" ..... but it was.

I put the 'phone down, left the kiosk and wondered at their nerve, the total order was 3d (1½p in new money) and I was expected to deliver it and invoice it also. The more I thought of it the more indignant I became, but then I remembered my last words to them as I left their office.

"No matter how little, I will deliver it personally within the hour." A promise is a promise and promises must be kept.

So I arrived at the travel agency fifteen minutes later with the box of paper clips.

"Thanks very much," the secretary said to me as cheerfully as before, "But before you go the Boss would like to see you in his office."

I entered the inner sanctum and was greeted by "I like a man who keeps his word, now we also want three desks, three chairs and a filing cabinet, can I have them tomorrow?"

It was like winning the pools. It was the equivalent of about the next eight weeks' wages and I assured him the furniture would be there the following day. I indulged in peas to go with my fish and chips that night as a celebration.

I was up bright and early the next day, loading up the furniture. It was no problem loading it up, with the help of the warehousemen, but as I drew up outside the travel agents on King Street it occurred to me that I was not going to be able to manhandle it in by myself.

It wasn't the thing to ask the customer to give me a lift. Humping in his own desks was definitely not on and I was reluctant to ask him. I stood at the kerb leaning on my car, eyeing the desks and waiting for inspiration.

"Hello, my son," came the cheery greeting in a familiar Scottish accent from behind me. I recognised the voice immediately and I turned to be greeted by the greatest goal scorer in the world at that time, Denis Law. He looked the picture of health, his blond mane shining, his smile as broad as ever.

Denis has always been great to me; I was still a groundstaff boy at Maine Road when he signed for Manchester City for a record £55,000 transfer fee from Huddersfield Town and I used to clean his boots. He was then transferred to Torino in Italy, but had not settled down in the land of the lira and had returned to England to link up with Manchester United. Even though our careers had taken off in the exact opposite direction to each other's—his rocketed skywards, mine plummeted downwards—whenever I saw him he was always cheery and friendly, the bigger the star the nicer the man.

Now we were here on King Street and I had the problem of my first-ever order to deliver for Fred Eyre Stationers.

Denis soon solved my problem for me by taking one end of desk as I took the other and we humped the gear in together.

My new clients must have thought I was a very successful businessman to have Britain's number one footballer working for him as a part-time delivery boy.

The next day completed my first week as an entrepreneur and thanks to the furniture order it had been a profitable week.

I had £129 14s 3d left of my £150 starting capital, most of my suppliers had granted me a monthly account with the usual warning, "Don't let me down with payment". I knew I had no intention of doing so, but others were understandably a little wary of this youngster and I had to pay cash when I dealt with them. I held no resentment to the suppliers who refused me my much needed credit, but I always, even to this day, put them to the bottom of my list of alternative suppliers when I am ready to place big orders. I always consider those first who helped my when I needed them most.

I was very pleased with my first week's trading but at the back of my mind was the thought that it was only the furniture order that had pulled me through and I wouldn't get one of those every week.

The next week went pretty much the same way, with many, many refusals.

"Please can I see the Manager?"

"Dave, there's a kid here selling stationery," he shouted over a partition. "Tell him to piss off" came the subtle reply.

My unseen, smooth talker, unknown to me was one of my Waterpark squad of Jewish players and a couple of weeks later he said, after I had put them through a particularly gruelling session, "I believe you have got your own stationery business. I use plenty, come and see me tomorrow," and handed me a card which I stuffed into my tracksuit pocket.

I made it my first call the next morning and obviously remembered the place from my previous visit as I climbed the stairs and told the same chap;-

"I'm the fellow you told to piss off a fortnight ago. Your Boss now wants to open an account." They are still with me today and every time I take a further major step forward in my business, Stuart Diner always reminds me, "You've come a long way, kid, since I threw you out of my office".

This day, however, it was just one of a dozen knock backs as I kept battling away. Eventually, somebody ordered a typewriter and I had made a profit for the week again ..... but if I hadn't sold the typewriter! I won't sell one of those every week!

This is how it went for months, every week a struggle but one big sale pulling me out each time, until I began to accept the fact that if you stick at it, there will always be something to pull you through.

My rule when I started was, as soon as my original £150 was gone I would quit. I had no overdraft and was using my Dad's principles of life in my business, "Only spend what you've got". It got pretty near the watermark at times, the lowest was £30 16 shillings, but I always just managed to keep my head above water, and all the time my list of customers was growing, and every single week I managed to make a profit. This went on for the next eighteen months. During this time the Boss of a big stationers in Manchester offered to buy me out completely and I could have a nice bank balance and a top job in his company. I was flattered and tempted but stuck to my guns and said "No thanks"!

twenty-five

1969 – MY YEAR

1969 was to be the big year in my life although it didn't get off to a flying start. I was still enjoying life at Chorley and had won a couple of medals with them. The brand new Northern Premier League was formed and Chorley was a founder member and I played in the first ever Northern Premier League game—a 0-0 draw with Altrincham. I was participating in one of our Thursday night training sessions when I challenged our big keeper Ronnie Fairbrother for a cross in a little five-a-side game.

It was an innocuous challenge but our arms locked together and I felt my shoulder lift out. My shoulder blade was jutting out somewhere behind my left ear, the pain was the worst that I could imagine, much worse than when I did my leg in and it was with extreme difficulty that I was escorted to hospital in Chorley.

I reached the outpatients at ten to eight in the evening and at ten past eleven two Pakistani doctors were still trying to wrestle the dislocated shoulder back into its socket.

Eventually there was a locking sound and it flew back into place. The three of us slumped back in our chairs, me sweating with pain, and the two of them sweating with the sheer effort of the bout, two falls or one submission!

The joy I felt as it clanked back to where it belonged was indescribable. My arm was put in a sling and I was told "Stay off work for four weeks, then come back and have the sling taken off''. They must be joking. I couldn't afford to stay off work for four minutes let alone four weeks and the next morning, usual time, I was off on my rounds driving one handed, steering with my right hand and just about steadying the wheel with the fingers of my left hand as I reached quickly across myself to change gear and snatch the wheel back again.

Reckless, but it was either that or no food.

So I had to keep working. If I stopped the whole business ceased, because as well as the buying and selling during the day I also typed the invoices and attended to the accounts in the evenings and dealt with any correspondence. This, in fact, went on for five years, during which time I never had one single day off, which was partly luck, I never even got flu during this time, and partly design because we had no holidays either but I was loving the work, even though it was hard. Every day was like a holiday.

My first 'phone call of the day to my Mother, the first when I was suffering the 'slings and arrows of outrageous misfortune' produced good dividends.

"Pace Advertising have phoned," she informed me. "They want 40 reams of foolscap duplicating paper before lunchtime."

This was a very nice order, quite a lot of money involved. Forty reams comes packed ten in a carton, and with plenty of effort a man can just about hoist it up onto his shoulder and stagger in with it, so under normal circumstances it would take four journeys from the car to Pace's office on the fourth floor of this building to complete the delivery.

But this time the circumstances were not normal. I wouldn't be able to manage a carton with my arm in a sling so I would have to open them up and take a box in at a time and make 40 trips from my car up to the fourth floor. "Thank goodness there is a lift," I thought, as I began my first trip with my first box.

"Sorry lift out of order." The sign was there for all to see but I refused to believe it as I pressed the button frantically; but, yes, it was the awful truth. I had 40 journeys up eight flights of stairs to reach the fourth floor if I was to delivery my order. No use looking at it, get stuck in ..... my legs were wobbling an hour and a quarter later!

The business continued to prosper and Judith and I were eagerly awaiting the birth of our first child. I was really excited as she was admitted to hospital.

The next day, 1st February, two days before my own birthday, Suzanne was born and the first time I saw her little face was the greatest moment in my life. I was thrilled three years later when my son (I always wanted a son) Steven was born, but nothing could ever compare with my feelings as I looked at Suzanne for the first time.

I left the hospital with my Mother a happy and proud Father and resolved to make the business go even better now that I had this extra mouth to feed.

So I doubled my efforts and by June the sun was shining and business was good as I trekked around the town and bumped into Mr Muir again.

"Are you wantin' a shop?" he inquired in the familiar accent.

I had always wanted a shop ..... to play for City, to play for England, to have a son and to own a shop, my life's ambitions.

I'd sort of accomplished the first, no chance now for the second, although my innersoles did! Still time for the third and now being offered the fourth.

Mr Muir was offering me the little shop on Booth Street from where I'd bought my scrapbook years previously, and I really fancied it, but as always the money!

"I want £450, but I want it straight away, no messing about, 450 smackers."

I just about had that amount of money, but a shop needed completely stocking out with all office requirements and as always if I was intending to go into anything I only wanted to do it in the correct way, no half measure. I would sooner turn the opportunity down rather than not do it properly.

I said I would let him know and he very kindly said that if

I wanted to sit in the shop for a day to view the proceedings I could and I took him up on his offer.

The Booth Street shop was very secondary to his big one in St Peter's Square and I could tell Mr Muir just couldn't be bothered with it any more. The shelves were sparsely stocked, it didn't look good stock to me. The young lad who worked there was a nice boy but lacked interest, and no thought seemed to have gone into the layout, but I felt inwardly excited as I began my day's observation.

I perched myself in a little corner of this tiny basement premises to await developments.

The amount of traffic entering the shop amazed me. There was a steady stream of customers coming down the stairs, making their way to the counter, to be politely told whatever it was they required was out of stock and they made their way out again empty handed.

This went on all day until I began to wonder if I would ever see a coin make its way over the counter and into the till, but by lunch-time it hadn't happened.

After lunch, a local solicitor called in, strolled up to the counter and confidently asked "Do you have Bics?"

Now every stationer in the world stocks Bics. I could see a couple of boxes on the counter and so, at long last, I could witness a purchase being made, a transaction actually completed.

"Yes, we do," the assistant said smiling.

"I'll have a red one please," demanded the customer.

"Sorry, we only have blue or black," came the reply as another unsatisfied customer made his exit.

I'd seen enough, if I can't do better than that then I'll pack up.

I went straight to the bank, withdrew £450 and took it round to Mr Muir's to clinch the deal, for what was going to be the best piece of business I'll ever do in my life.

As the last week in June began I simply couldn't wait for Friday at five o'clock; Shaw's Stationers, as it was called, would close down and at one minute past I would begin my transformation.

I was fidgety all day long waiting for five o'clock to come and was sitting in my car opposite as I saw all the lights go out and as he locked the door I strolled over and took the key from him.

I had been building up stocks at Lancaster Avenue and I was joined that evening by my parents, my Auntie Sylvia and Uncle Arthur, their daughter Lynn, their next door neighbours, Mr & Mrs Crompton, and we literally took the place apart.

We began on Friday evening at 5.30, worked through until 2 am, were back in action at 7.30 next morning, Uncle Arthur and I simply journeying backwards and forwards from Lancaster Avenue to Booth Street with stock through to 2 am again, all day Sunday from 7.30 am to 3 am and I opened for business 5½ hours later at 8.30 on Monday morning 30th June 1969.

The little shop was sparkling, a super new sign erected, new shelving by courtesy of my Dad's handiwork, all packed out with brand new stock, new floor, old stands tarted up to look as good as new, a complete transformation.

Booth Street was literally blocked with all the rubbish we had thrown out and I felt confident that we had done a great job and that the way I had planned the shop to make the most of what little space we had was correct, and I was right.

From the very first day the shop was a roaring success. The takings were more in the first day than in the entire month prior to me taking over, I was on a winner here. It was a feeling I had never known before, one of absolute confidence in the knowledge that I knew exactly what I was doing, knew where I was going, and barring any unforeseen catastrophes I knew inwardly that I was on the threshold of something good. It was up to me from now on to make something happen from this small beginning.

I usually worked from six o'clock in the morning at the shop until I closed at six o'clock in the evening.

This wasn't exactly by choice, our daughter Suzanne simply did not sleep ..... ever since the day she was born until the age of three she never slept for more than three hours any night. From the age of three until five she was a little better, averaging about five hours a night, and now she is a young lady we can't get her to get up!

Invariably Judith and I were still up at about five-thirty in the morning still trying to tire her out, so it was a waste of time me going back to bed — I simply went to work and completed all my paper work with only the milkman to keep me company.

Things got so bad with Suzanne we took her to doctors, specialists, but nothing could be done, we just had to wait for her to grow out of it.

In the meantime we had to send her to my Mother's for a week every few months in order that we could get some sleep. Still she made sure I was never late for work.

On the soccer scene 1969 was to be a good year also. I was, amazingly, back with a Football League Club. Bradford Park Avenue were going through a particularly sticky time and asked me to sign.

They needed experienced players, but had no money to obtain any from other league clubs so they began searching non-league.

The Chairman of the club, an eccentric businessman, Mr Metcalf, was based in Manchester, knew of my pedigree and decided I was the man for them—I said he was eccentric!

So I went to see the Manager Don McAlman and pledged with him to get Bradford Park Avenue out of the Fourth Division. This I succeeded in doing ..... I took them into the Northern Premier League!

I was only at the club a short time but I played under four managers, they had a turnstile on the Manager's door instead of hinges.

That same evening I played against Notts County and whilst strolling to the ground I bought the local newspaper to find that I was to play right full-back. I'd played in many positions during my ten years as a pro but never at full-back, so it was going to be extra difficult, back amongst the full-time pros again and also in a strange position.

I stood outside the dressing-room for as long as I could, chatting to a former team mate Alan Smith, not really wanting to go in the dressing-room amongst all the full timers, who must have been wondering who was going to be the occupant of the only shirt left hanging on a peg, the number two shirt.

Ten past seven, I couldn't leave it any longer, fifteen minutes before we were due on the field was very late anyway, so I took a deep breath and walked in.

The sight that met me left me speechless. The atmosphere was familiar to all the dozens of others I'd been in, clothes hanging everywhere, tie ups strewn around, plasters, smell of oil and liniment, but no noise, all very quiet, the players were all sitting watching 'This is Your Life' on television. They were stripped ready for the game but their eyes were glued to the set, Notts County were a mile from their thoughts.

I stood there transfixed; then I looked up at the set, I remember Pat Phoenix was on, I'm not sure if she was a guest or the life subject, but I then pulled myself together and quickly got changed.

The referee's bell rang to signal we should make our way to the field but nobody moved a muscle until the refrains from the 'This is Your Life' music died down, then we all got to our feet and descended the stairs, through the bathroom and out onto the pitch. Unbelievable!

I enjoyed the game immensely and felt I played well. I was really at home at full-back and only wished I'd moved there years earlier. I was always facing the play, I could see the whole picture and knew I had found a new position and I stayed a full-back until I retired ten years later.

As usual I spent most of my time captaining the reserve team but was thoroughly enjoying my life back in the 'Bigtime'. However, Don McAlman soon lost his job and was followed by Ron Lewin, Frank Tomlinson and Tony Leighton. They used to write the Manager's name on his office door in chalk at Park Avenue! ..... with a wet sponge hanging beside it!!

Ron, of the old school tie and plum-in-the-mouth brigade, looked down his nose at all us 'scrubbers' who couldn't play. He always left us with the impression that he was used to dealing with better-class players ..... He probably was!!

Frank Tomlinson I'd never heard of. He was from Manchester ..... from Manchester and I'd never heard of him, it was inconceivable. He was a steward at a social club. I think somebody must have told Mr Metcalf he was a manager of a club and he must have thought they meant a football club and he gave him the job, but he showed great judgement by selecting me for the first team away to high flying Swansea.

Money was always a problem at Bradford; George Brigg, the secretary, used to have an enormous Alsatian dog in his office. I'm sure it was as a deterrent to stop players collecting their wages. It was always a problem getting paid, usually I didn't even bother attempting to collect mine.

This particular week I played away at Middlesbrough on Tuesday and chased Irish International Johnny Crossan around Ayresome Park, arriving back home at three o'clock in the morning to be in the shop three hours later around six-thirty in the morning.   I then left for Swansea in a blizzard on Friday lunch-time, stayed Friday night at a hotel in Mumbles, got hammered by Swansea the next day, tried to mark Welsh International Len Allchurch without much success, arrived home one o'clock on Sunday morning, total pay for my endeavours and days off away from business, nothing, not one penny ..... they make a fortune these Football League players!

I had now been with the club for three months and they said they would like me to stay but couldn't find the obligatory signing on fee that they had to give me.

I told them that I didn't want it, but the Football League stated that I had to have it whether I wanted it or not, plus the same amount had to be paid to them. The total was five hundred pounds and the club simply did not have the cash, so until they paid up I was not allowed to play in the league team, only the reserves.

This was bad news for me, I wanted to stay, the club wanted me to stay (or said they did) but I couldn't play because of this rule. There was nothing I could do.

Eventually they asked me if I would play for the reserve team in the mid-week league and be manager of the Youth Team in the intermediate league on Saturdays. I agreed, and so, became a Manager for the first time at the age of twenty-five. I was promised wages for my double job but rarely saw any.

It was useful early experience handling young players and also their Dads and it stood me in good stead for future years plus I was still playing in a good standard, so I was fairly happy and content. At the end of the season Park Avenue were forced to apply for re-election and were not successful so were relegated to the Northern Premier League, a familiar stamping ground for me, so I was a useful person to retain on the staff for the next season.

I used to give lifts in my car back to Manchester to many youngsters and this evening after a game at Roker Park against Sunderland, I dropped about seven of these young hopefuls off in Piccadilly, I slowed down, they each jumped out of my car and ran off to catch their respective buses home. "Tarra"! each one said as they sprinted away. If they had played well they would have been too tired to sprint!

Only one boy, a slim, fresh-faced lad with a mass of blond curly hair paused and said "Thank you very much for the lift", and I watched him dash off to catch up with the others. On the strength of this alone I offered the lad a job at Fred Eyre Stationers when he left school a few weeks later and my judgement proved correct because Geoff Priestner eventually became a director of the company. I may not have been a shrewd judge of football talent, but I certainly knew a good stationer when I saw one!!

twenty–six

NEARLY AS MANY BUSINESSES AS FOOTBALL CLUBS

My instinct regarding the possibilities of the shop in Booth Street was fast proving to be correct, but all the while I was aware of another two stationers directly opposite me at number six, who, whilst they didn't have a shop front, seemed to do extraordinarily well.

Whenever a supplier delivered a big order to us, I would watch in amazement as he would then deliver twice or three times as much to them.

This had to be investigated further.

This was easier said than done, they were like invisible men. I never saw them. How they managed to do so well in business I couldn't imagine, but all of this stock constantly arriving must be being sold to somebody.

Eventually I discovered the two businesses, H. H. Ashworth Ltd and Holiday Taylor Ltd, were owned by Mr Leech, a man who looked in his sixties and he was assisted by Mr Winstanley, probably in his forties, and Mr Brannan looked after the accounts of these well-established businesses and he was in his seventies! Not a very good half-back line but certainly formidable opposition on the business side.

The town wasn't big enough for both of us so I thought if I can't wipe them out I'd better buy them out, but my overtures fell on deaf ears.

Soon afterwards though, fate struck Mr Leech a cruel blow.

He suffered a heart attack and couldn't carry on the business so he rang me and offered to sell and I paid £15,000 to acquire the businesses of H. H. Ashworth and Holiday Taylor to go with the Shaw and Company shop and my own little Fred Eyre Stationers that I began with and I thought at that point I had reached the ultimate.

On the football side, Frank Tomlinson had been replaced by Tony Leighton, a blunt Yorkshireman who was a brave centre forward in his days with Huddersfield Town, Doncaster and Bradford City. Now nearing the end of his playing days he swept into Park Avenue with the finesse of a charging rhino.

I didn't like his style, screaming, shouting, abusing his players; I used to sit back with a resigned look on my face as he slated each player in turn. I knew I would be on my travels again soon.

Tony, sadly for his family and friends, died from illness not long afterwards, which was a tragedy for such a fit and virile man. He had boundless energy and was liked by many, but not really by me, and I was off to join Rossendale United.

Rossendale with due respect to them, had for many years been regarded as a joke in their league. That was until Les Rigby took control and turned the club inside out.

Les, a big burly ex-centre half for Lytham, knew non-league football inside out, from A to Z, knew every player, no matter how obscure, his strengths, his weaknesses, even what he had for breakfast. Les impressed me immensely, and in fact still does. He's a physical training instructor at Wigan Technical College and I regard him as a close friend, but this day he was my prospective Manager as he prepared to smooth talk me into signing for his team, that had the previous season romped away with the Cheshire League.

"Can't see you getting into a great side like this," he 'coaxed' me, "but I would like you in my squad. The money is low also."

"How low," I enquired.

"Sod all," he said. "Until I release somebody, then you can have his wages."

"Sod all," I mused.

"That **is** pretty low, Les."

But I signed nevertheless and I'm glad I did.

I loved it at Rossendale. The ground had seen better days, the changing accommodation left a lot to be desired but the players were great.

We were a bunch of misfits, me included, but Les, with great perception, saw despite our various failings what each individual had; we all had one thing in common, we could all play. We all had skill, other clubs had not been able to harness it, but Les knew exactly what he wanted and utilised all our assets to make a great team and I was proud to be part of it.

We did well in the league again, finishing runners up. The reason we did not win it I feel is because we also surpassed ourselves in a few cup competitions always playing teams higher than ourselves and always winning whether we were drawn at home or away. This took its toll and we dropped a couple of silly points near the end to finish runners up.

We also became that season's giant killers in the FA Cup, reaching the Fourth round before being beaten by Bolton Wanderers 1-4.

I had played in the earlier rounds and helped us reach this momentous occasion but as in the past I got a sickener as we played a 'nothing' game the week before. I went in for another reckless tackle. I knew instinctively that I was in trouble as soon as I made the tackle, and stood on one leg to see my other leg wafting about from side to side in the night breeze. Not backwards and forwards as everybody else's does, but loosely just swinging from side to side as if hanging on a thread.

I knew it was a long job so I didn't even wait for the game to stop, I simply hopped to the touchline, hopped up the tunnel into the dressing-room and out of the game for twelve weeks and obviously out of Saturday's big game with Bolton Wanderers.

I was forced to watch the game from the touchline ironically with broken leg victim David Crompton, our flying left winger who is now Youth Team Coach at Wigan Athletic, as we ripped into our famous opponents from the kick-off. The game had been switched to Gigg Lane, Bury's ground, to accommodate the 17,000 crowd and whilst driving to the ground, my pal, John Clay, an inside forward who was with me at City, was obviously thinking I was feeling a little bit left out of things so he turned to me on the coach and said: "If I score I will come racing over to the box so you can join in the celebrations". "OK", I smiled at his optimism, but with seventeen minutes gone he broke through, past centre half Paul Jones, drew keeper Charlie Wright off his line and calmly slotted it past him for the opening goal. The crowd went wild as he, true to his word, came charging across to me on our jubilant bench. It was a nice moment and even though we eventually crumbled to a Roy Greaves hat-trick, the boys did themselves proud and gave us all a day to remember.

I was back for all the other cup finals and won a hatful of trophies with Rossendale. One of the finals had to be postponed an hour before the kick-off because the weather suddenly changed, and unfortunate though it was, the referee was perfectly correct to postpone the game.

On hearing this one of the Rossendale committee calmly walked into the referee's room and remonstrated with him.

"You cannot call this game off referee, it is totally out of the question. The game simply has to be played because we have ordered the pies."

It was great at Rossy!

While I was at Rossendale I realised what a great boost to my career the substitute rule had been.

I spent so much time on the bench I considered becoming a magistrate ..... when we used to arrive at away grounds the players invariably went to inspect the pitch to see which studs they would wear. I simply inspected the bench, was it wooden? or a chair, maybe a cushion provided if it was a really luxurious ground. After games the other lads would be having treatment for blistered feet, I was having the same treatment for my backside.

The finest selection of a substitute I ever saw in my life

happened during this period; we didn't have a big squad of players and the team was so hard hit by injuries that we only had eleven fit players for the game, plus the spare goalkeeper. It was decided that because we were struggling for players, the keeper would be the substitute and the opposition wouldn't think anything was wrong when twelve of us trotted out, and the Manager just prayed that nobody got injured.

The game had only been in motion about three minutes when somebody did get injured ..... the goalkeeper broke his hand and was promptly replaced by our substitute. As he was donning the green jersey, I could hear our opponents telling each other to get ripped into this substitute between the posts. "Get plenty of crosses in;" "Test him with high balls etc." The 'novice' proceeded to give a highly polished and competent display of goalkeeping much to the astonishment of the opposition and it was only at the end of the game when the match had been won that we let them into the secret of the substitute.

'I had a feeling our keeper may get injured so I had another goalie as sub just in case," crowed our Manager.

Another classic was a game where we had been given a real roasting by our opponents. It was a day when nothing seemed to go right and midway through the second half we saw the substitute warming up and the first time the ball went out of play we all glanced towards the touchline to see who the unlucky player was who was to be brought off.

The trainer was standing on the line holding up the card with the big number eleven on it.

"Who me?" shouted our outside left towards the bench "No! the whole bloody lot of you!" retorted our Manager.

Rossendale United also provided my first soccer trip abroad. Les Rigby organised a fantastic trip to New York in 1972. I'd never been abroad before and it was the first of many more trips which brought me 46 games in twenty-one countries around the world.

They had all been marvellous but the first one is always special.

We played six games in and around the New York area,

Orange Grove, New Jersey; Greenwich Village, Hartford; Connecticut; Falls River, Philadelphia; and a game against New York Cosmos at 'The Hosfra Stadium'. This gave me a unique opportunity to witness the progress of American soccer during the next five years, because I am one of the few people to play against them at their outset at 'The Hosfra' in 1972 and then again in 1977 when they had advanced at an alarming rate, after the signing of Pele, to their present pinnacle at the mighty Giant Stadium in New Jersey.

It was a tremendous experience for me to lead my team out into this huge bowl-shaped arena with its gigantic scoreboard welcoming us to 'The Cosmos'.

The ground shone like a new pin, the dressing-rooms resembled the most luxurious Swiss clinic. Moving staircases on the exterior of the ground took the spectators to their seats. The artificial Astro turf was even and looked like a subbuteo board, and the all-seater stadium, which holds 77,000, is set in its own grounds surrounded by a giant car park to hold thousands and thousands of cars. It is a breathtaking sight as you drive towards it and view the stadium in the distance and think that within the hour you will be performing there.

That is progress, because my first game against The Cosmos was this day in June 1972 on the University campus. It was a nice little ground with good facilities but nothing to compare with where they were moving to in the future.

The game was memorable for me because in a 3-1 win I scored all the goals. Not bad for a left back, but they were all penalties!

It was strange how many penalties we were given in these matches abroad, we seemed to be awarded one almost every other game; I accepted the responsibility and happily slotted every one in.

All the games on this tour were memorable, the first one was at Jones Beach, New York. The pitch was next to this famous beach with its white sands and rolling waves. At the end of the game we forsook the dressing-room facilities and chose instead to bathe in the sea, still wearing our kit. We kicked off within an hour of reaching Kennedy Airport. We had flown half-way round the world, or so it seemed, struggled through customs with our luggage to be told we were kicking off within the hour, so, luggage and all, we arrived at the ground for the game; we didn't even have time for a wash before we were lining up to kick off in 95°.

It was like a furnace and took me quite a time to catch my breath, but it was a tremendous game which in spite of our taking an early lead, we eventually lost 3-4. Jet lag we told everybody.

My partner at full-back on this trip was David Brooks, a well-known local amateur player who is a very successful solicitor in his private life. He is about 5ft. 5in. but he would be 6ft. 2in. if his legs were straight, has red hair like me, only not as much, and we looked a fiery combination. I think we complemented each other very well, he provided the thrust—he is very quick, marks his winger like a leech, wins nearly all his tackles and then passes the ball into touch! I provided the guile, a little on the slow side, but read the game well and was a good passer of the ball. If we each also possessed the other's assets we would be great players.

However, I thought we were a good partnership and we went on to play hundreds of games together all over the world.

When I was appointed coach at Wigan Athletic a few years later, the Boss, Ian McNiell, said I could have an assistant, provided he was honest, had a good character, had a good knowledge of the game and had been a good player himself. I said I didn't know anybody like that, so could I have Dave Brooks!

He agreed and we are still partners. The high spot of his career was when he played in front of The Duke of Edinburgh and The Prince of Wales ..... he's also played in front of other pubs in the Manchester area but these are the best two.

Back home, my private life continued to prosper, business was still improving. I had endured many major national crises and still come up smiling but there were one or two more still to come.

There had been three big increases in purchase tax, each increase meant big problems for me. This was eventually replaced by VAT, which caused immense worry. The pound was devalued, we had the three day week, people had to work three days, on the instructions of the Government. This was a blow to some of my mates because prior to this they only worked two days!

There were 'black-outs' when the miners went on strike, we never knew when we were going to be plunged into darkness, which is obviously a problem for a shopkeeper, plus all the heating and electricity went off without warning. This meant if the electric till happened to be closed when we were cut off we couldn't open it again to give customers their change. They still came in to buy, even in the dark.

Also there was decimalisation, the biggest problem of all. I had done everything possible to ensure a smooth change-over but the success of it depended on me being there. The day before the big day, I was struck down with glandular fever and was really ill for a fortnight. It had to be bad for me to miss the big day .....the day that was going to put Britain on its knees. It still hasn't recovered in my opinion from this grave mistake.

But I had survived these history-making moments. We had moved house a couple of years previously from Radcliffe to Whitefield, a very classy area about three miles away, and were now looking for another larger house because five weeks before my American trip my son Steven Frederick Eyre was born.

This was another momentous occasion in my life, because I had got used to having a daughter and was convinced that we would have another girl, I was both surprised and overjoyed when I was told it was a boy.

My first sight of him was a big disappointment, however. I was quite taken aback. Suzanne had looked so perfect and lovely that I thought all babies looked that way, so I was shocked to see Steven, wrinkled and yellow, lying in his cot; it quite upset me. Thankfully he soon pulled himself round and is now a fine young boy, who looks a very talented young footballer, playing for his school at a record early age ..... Oh! no not an action replay!

We eventually moved to a lovely Georgian house in Worsley, a very salubrious area of Manchester, a little in the country but close enough for me to travel into Manchester in a matter of minutes. I love it in Worsley and don't think I will ever leave the area.

The main competition to Fred Eyre Stationers was a large shop round the corner on Princess Street, a main thoroughfare running alongside the Town Hall.

It was old established and situated in this prime position. The owner, Mr Crichton, was not a young man, so I made an appointment to see him with a view to purchasing his business.

There were comparatively few snags and soon a deal was completed and I obtained this prestigious establishment for £25,000.

In effect I now owned five stationary businesses all within a radius of about 50 yards. It seemed rather a bizarre situation even to me, but each one was successful so I simply carried on.

Buying stock for five companies enabled me to obtain the best possible terms from my suppliers and any extra profits I made in this way I attempted to share with my customers by keeping my prices as reasonable as possible.

Company number six came my way with the purchase of a small stationery business in Poynton, near Stockport. I immediately closed this down and absorbed it into the other five.

Six companies now owned I felt that this was enough, because I didn't want to lose the personal touch and service that had always been my trademark, so I entered a period of consolidation, happy and contented with my lot.

I was not happy and contented with my football, however. I was now 30, the age when everybody says you are finished as a player, and I believed them. It is an attitude of mind and I must admit that my mind was invariably focused on my business, which is not surprising because it was producing lucrative rewards, and not on my football.

I occasionally missed training sessions, which is not like me at all. I wasn't the fittest but I was the most reliable; this was due to the extra work involved in running all six companies and it occurred to me that it would be a good idea to finish playing and if possible remain in the game in some capacity, as a hobby.

twenty-seven

JUST MANAGING

Two of my closest friends, Bobby Smith from way back in my Ducie Avenue days, and George Smith, a lovable Irish goalkeeper from my days at Buxton, each secured a job in football at this time. Bob became coach and subsequently Manager, the youngest in the Football League at the time, of Bury Football Club and George became Manager of Cheshire League side Stalybridge Celtic. Both of them recognising talent when they saw it, each offered me a job on their staff.

In view of my business commitments and the fact that I wanted to take things easy ..... I accepted both jobs ..... I trained the Stalybridge lads on Tuesday and Thursday evenings but took charge of the Bury Central League team on Saturdays. I've never heard of such an arrangement before but it worked well.

The Bury set-up was great, there were many promising lads in the team who went on to become big names. There were games at Anfield, where we pitted our wits against Ray Kennedy, Terry McDermott, Chris Lawler and many more. Old Trafford, Stoke City, I enjoyed being back amongst the full-time pros, but I didn't really like the atmosphere at Gigg Lane, apart, of course, from my old pal, Bob.

I had acquired myself a Rolls Royce by this time, with a personalised SFE 1 number plate (for when I received my Knighthood!) had all the trappings of a successful young man, and it seemed to be resented by The Chairman and The Secretary and they were at this time not very pleasant towards me. Their attitude changed years later when I think they realised I simply loved the game and was just helping my mate in his first job in management, but nevertheless it made me feel uncomfortable.

The atmosphere was just the opposite at homely Stalybridge. George Smith is a smashing person, a chatterbox but a very hard-working manager who had the utmost respect of his players and he had my respect too.

After a short while I decided I could do without the derisory looks from the Secretary each time I went to collect the few bob (literally) that Bob promised me for my expenses.

I didn't do the job for the money, far from it, but his reluctance to hand it over really annoyed me and in the end I decided to concentrate solely on Stalybridge Celtic.

I still did some midweek scouting for Bury but only as a favour to Bob.

I was sponge man at Stalybridge, rubbing the legs and generally looking after the needs of the players and I thoroughly enjoyed it; I helped George Smith with the training but he was definitely the Boss and I wouldn't have had it any other way.

Eventually George's talents were recognised by the people of Iceland and he was off to this iced backwater to further his career.

I was ready to leave also, because I really worked for George, not Stalybridge Celtic, and was preparing to do so when I was offered the job as Manager.

I was very flattered but declined immediately; to be a Manager of a Football Club was the last thing I wanted.

However, we all have our weak spots and my vanity was pricked when the players held a meeting and presented a deputation to the board of Directors saying they wanted me to be the Manager.

This was simply too much for my ego and I finally accepted the post ..... and regretted it from almost the first minute.

I have always been very professional in everything I have ever tried to do and never needed to be carried around and wet nursed in the way that George had done with some of the players.

It was George's way to do absolutely everything for his players; he even instructed them on what to eat, even though half of them sank about six pints of beer a night in their spare time!

I wasn't prepared to do this. I pinned a team-sheet on the notice board with the time the coach would be leaving typed on, and didn't expect to be aroused from my slumbers by a call from a telephone box at 2.00 in the morning to be asked "What time does the coach go on Saturday?"

Some of the players came to me about every stupid little thing. They were much, much worse than famous pros who were household names whom I had dealt with in the past.

I really disliked the job but didn't have the heart to resign after such a short time.

The results on the field were quite good and I sold 20 year-old Eammon O'Keefe, to Plymouth Argyle for a reported club record fee, which helped to pay for the floodlights; so in my eleven weeks in charge my record was quite good and we made a huge profit. He eventually moved on to Everton and became a Republic of Eire International.

The day I sold Eammon, Plymouth Argyle were staying in the Midlands for a week so we drove down to Coventry City's ground, where Coventry's Youth Team were playing Ipswich Town that afternoon, for a rendezvous with Argyle Manager, ex-England goalkeeper, Tony Waiters, to talk terms.

We exchanged pleasantries and agreed the fee, then simply to make conversation I remarked to Tony "I suppose it is necessary to adopt this policy of buying young players and grooming them because Devon isn't really a good catchment area for young players like say Manchester or Liverpool. They don't exactly grow wild in your area do they?" He then amazed me by replying "Oh, I don't know about that, our left back Colin Sullivan has been known to lose his temper on occasions."

Good Luck Eammon!

Judith, meantime, had been having serious problems with her throat; we had tried every cure except a rope or a razor, so she was admitted to hospital for an operation.

Six businesses, two young children and a football team to look after, with a wife in hospital, it was just the excuse I needed, so I immediately handed in my resignation.

I could have coped but I didn't want to; it was accepted, it said in the press, "with regret".

I bumped into one of the directors a few weeks later who casually informed me "We would have sacked you anyway!"

"Thanks very much! Oh! by the way my wife's recovering nicely ..... thanks for asking." I was glad to be away; George Smith was the main difference, I loved it while George was there and hated it when he wasn't.

I then came across a man called Chris Davies, who obviously thought I was "too young to die" and that I still had something to offer as a player. He invited me to join his team, a select band of amateur players who toured abroad every close season under the banner 'Manchester AFC' and played in tournaments all round the world each summer. He said they could do with somebody with my experience to play in the team and our games in Spain and Morocco whetted my appetite again and I thoroughly enjoyed it all. We were treated like kings, escorted round the Palace in Morocco and generally had a fine time.

Chris Davies is without doubt one of the nicest, charming men I have ever met; if it is possible he is too nice, always prepared to think the best of people, just the opposite to me, who is always prepared to think the worst!

He has done more than anybody I know to promote local amateur soccer and is one of the game's finest administrators. His trips are always superbly organised and the one trip to Spain and Morocco was followed by tours to Jamaica, Haiti, Cuba, The Bahamas, The United States (many times), Canada, Barbados, Trinidad, Tobago, France, Belgium and most of the European countries. I love to travel and I always did my best to ensure that Chris selected me for the next trip until the day came when I had to admit I was just too old; it was a sad day for me and hopefully for Chris too.

twenty-eight
THE WORLD IS
MY LOBSTER

Jamaica was a place I found to be a little frightening. It is a lovely island but I sensed an undercurrent of violence running through the whole place.

The team were allocated three luxurious houses next door to one another on Patterson Avenue in Montego Bay; each had its own swimming pool, with a maid, cook and gardener to each villa.

We were perched high above Montego Bay and the view was breathtaking, our first game was in Montego Bay, which we won after we had first of all helped the officials to remove a stubborn cow from the pitch which simply refused to move.

When I saw the size of the player I was marking I thought it had come back on the field again!

From there we moved to Kingston, the Capital of Jamaica, and I felt even more hostility towards us.

The night before the game I was sitting in a cafe having a bedtime cup of coffee to quench an everlasting thirst, before retiring for the night. I was sitting with Dave Brooks chatting about the forthcoming game when a local Jamaican youth sidled up to me, gave a quick glance over each shoulder and whispered to me from out of the corner of his mouth

"Say man, do you want coke?"

I looked up, startled to be approached in this strange place.

"No thanks, I just ordered this coffee"! I replied naively.

He retreated scratching his head, obviously thinking how stupid these Englishmen are.

My fears regarding the violence were confirmed as we stood in the tunnel waiting to take the field at the National Stadium, a fantastic complex, where the Commonwealth Games had been held and where Smokin' Joe Frazier was knocked out by George Foreman when he lost the Heavyweight Championship of the World.

We could have done with him this night on our side because before we even reached the pitch we were subjected to a deluge of spit as the crowd proceeded to spit all over us as we took the field.

We had two players sent off, our goalkeeper, Roy Davies carried off, and the rest of us told to "bugger off" as we literally battled our way to an honorable 0-0 draw.

Even with the depleted team I would have died rather than let them score and was delighted that under the circumstances they hadn't won. I was disappointed that we hadn't won either but I'm glad they didn't.

It was midnight as we left the stadium and we faced a six-hour coach journey through the jungle back to Montego Bay. The journey out had been horrendous, up mountains, over bumpy roads, narrow bends, over streams and after the efforts of the game I simply couldn't bear even to think about it, so I decided along with 'Brooky' to invest in an overnight stay at an hotel and a flight back to Montego Bay in the morning.

I paid for this little perk myself, of course, but I thought I deserved a bit of luxury after working hard all my life, and even though I felt I really should have stayed with the team, I enjoyed a night's sleep instead.

The following morning as I tucked into a hearty breakfast I was informed quite matter of factly that a man had been murdered outside my bedroom window whilst I slept like a baby. Perhaps I should have gone with the team after all!

After the treatment we incurred in Kingston some of the players were a little reluctant to venture into the unknown of Communist Cuba and a meeting was held in my bedroom. I was alarmed to see that when a show of hands was asked for half were in favour of going and half were not.

I thought we may be in serious trouble if we went back on our word and did not go and finally persuaded the doubters to make the trip.

CUBA

It's a good job we decided to go, because there was a big reception party waiting to meet us at the airport in Havana, but even this couldn't cut us through all the red tape.

There were dreary black and white pictures in shabby frames of Fidel Castro and Che Guevara all over the airport, and endless military men in faded khaki uniforms wandering about sporting guns and grim faces.

Finally we were escorted through to our coach, which was even more ramshackle than the aircraft we had just left; it wasn't as good as the aeroplanes used to take holidaymakers for a flip around Blackpool Tower, and I'm sure it had an outside toilet!

The thing that struck me most as we drove through deserted drab streets was the lack of advertising boards. The boards were all there but they didn't say "Beanz Meanz Heinz" or "My Goodness My Guinness" but simply reminded the inhabitants of Havana what a great life it is in Cuba and how much Mr Castro was doing for his people.

We reached the Hotel National on the tip of the coast. We could see Miami in the distance and thought how different things were only a few miles across the sea. The Hotel National is a huge place in poor repair and in need of a lot of restoration work doing on it. Only the first two floors were used and it was with a little trepidation that we made our way to our rooms.

I was in Cuba for three days and in all the time there I never ate one single scrap of food, it was absolutely appalling. Most of my time was spent walking the streets and sitting by the hotel pool, but not for long because the heat was unbearable.

Each time I left the hotel I was besieged by young boys asking me for chewing gum, an unknown commodity there, and by adults for my tee shirts and any other garment from the Western World.

My main hobby when I am abroad is scouring the local shops. I love going out on my own, looking for unusual objets d'art for our home and different styles and items of clothing for myself, Judith and the children, and things for my Mother and Father. I had no chance of doing this in Havana; there is no private enterprise whatsoever and we had to ask for the whole team to go en bloc to a state-owned shop to buy our gifts.

Even this was not as simple as it sounds; everything in Cuba is about five years behind in style to the Europeans and Americans—'Brooky's' suit was the height of fashion in Havana!

So we struggled to find anything suitable to bring back for our families, which was a shame because I am sure we will never go back there again.

The game itself was an eye opener. The Stadium Latin Americana was magnificent, a huge arena which seated about 50,000 people, and we were amazed to find it nearly full as we left the dressing-rooms.

It was only afterwards that we discovered that all sport is free in Cuba, so it was a free night out for the locals and they had not paid out any hard-earned pesos to see us in action.

Our opponents, the Cuban National Team, were a fine side and very fit and fast and they gave us a bit of a chasing. We were the first British team ever to have played in Cuba so we didn't know what to expect and they ripped into us from the kick-off.

The Cuban Television cameras viewed our every move, they were even in our dressing-room at half-time and also at the end of the game; it was a good job they couldn't speak English as we gave vent to our feelings in the dressing-room at the end.

During the game Cuba were awarded a penalty, and it was at this point that I was paid the greatest compliment I have ever had regarding my vast knowledge of the game.

As soon as the spot kick had been awarded our silver-haired goalkeeper, the extrovert Roy Davies, slowly walked from his goal-line to me standing on the edge of the penalty area and enquired "Which side does he put them?"

The only team to have ever played in Cuba and he expected me to know which side the number six puts his penalties!

I tried to keep my reputation intact by saying "Your left", and stood helpless as Roy took my usually sound advice and dived hopelessly the wrong way.

The look he gave me as he fished the ball out of the net was enough to kill me. Roy, always with good intentions, no matter what obscure corner of the world we were playing in, always came to me in the dressing-room before the game and with a slow shake of the head never failed to inform me that he had heard that the winger I was about to mark could 'catch pigeons'. Everywhere we went my winger apparently was a flyer. Great booster of confidence, my mate Roy! It was about time I made him suffer.

I was delighted to leave Cuba the next day after a conducted tour of building sites, schools being built, flats being constructed, all propaganda sights that we didn't want to see.

Whenever I, as the official spokesman, asked to be taken to see something of interest, where Fidel lived or anything of world-wide interest, it fell on deaf ears.

The nearest I got was a seat in the tank that Castro used on his triumphant journey through the town after he had overthrown the country. To do this I had to be accompanied by an armed guard who looked as though he was dying to receive an order from his superior to blow my head off.

HAITI

Haiti was a different proposition altogether. It is the poorest and most backward in the Western World. The majority of the inhabitants are negroes, the descendants of slaves. It has a long history of uprisings and revolutions, and they speak a

Creole dialect and practise Voodoo. The memory of Papa Doc and now his son Baby Doc dominate the island and there is an air of fear about the place, which I sensed as soon as we landed at the airport at Port-au-Prince.

My first sight as I left the airport was a huge poster adorning the nearest wall with a picture of myself and my team mates, advertising the forthcoming game; I realised then it was to be an important fixture.

We had a police escort from the airport to our hotel, motor-cycles flanking our three huge limousines with sirens blaring as we roared through the narrow streets and it was hard luck for anybody who couldn't get out of the way a bit sharpish.

One particularly vivid memory I have is of a woman, one of many, who was washing her hair in the gutter as the muddy, filthy water flowed along the side of the street. She was oblivious to the noise and commotion of our arrival and was on her hands and knees rinsing her hair as the car in which I was a passenger raced towards her. I was helpless in the front passenger seat as the wheels of the car actually ran over her hair, missing crushing her head by a couple of inches.

I had the distinct impression that human life counted for very little in Haiti.

The next morning we went to the Stade Silvio Cator Stadium for a training session and 3,000 people turned up simply to watch us train; a few discreet enquiries revealed that there is so little to do in Haiti that even our training session was re-garded as a big event.

The match itself was an eye opener, we played the National Champions Violette FC, who were very skilful players in their own right, but they reinforced their team for the occasion with three Argentinian Internationals, so they provided formidable oppositon.

The game was televised live in Haiti and also broadcast across the island. 'Brooky' being the only French-speaking player in the squad was in demand for after-match interviews, speaking on behalf of all the players.

I don't know what he told them but he certainly got the best reviews in the newspapers the next day!

NASSAU

Nassau in the Bahamas really was a beautiful place to play football, our games on this island kicked off at eight o'clock in the evening, just cool enough to enjoy the game.

I was interviewed one glorious sunny day for Bahama Radio outside our hotel on Paradise Island and as I answered the interviewer's many questions I could see over his shoulder a huge sign saying "Welcome to Paradise" and remember thinking how right that was.

The games were highly competitive and thoroughly enjoyable; we played their League Champions and a Representative XI of the whole League. I was happy with my form, even though I wasn't getting any younger, and nicked in with a couple of my usual penalties.

The opposition was well coached and organised because there were a number of ex-professionals from Britain out there passing on their knowledge to the locals.

From there we flew across to Miami to take part in a tournament with a team from Peru, one from Honduras, one from Haiti and ourselves.

The heat again was a main problem; each team played each other over a long weekend, so we played a match every day in 92° heat in the middle of the day.

We acquitted ourselves very well under the circumstances and came an honourable runner up to Haiti, who received the trophy.

I played games in many parts of America and have loved every one of my trips.

Each visit to the 'land of opportunity' convinces me that we are slipping further and further behind in this country. The service and value for money is much superior to ours in Great Britain, I have found.

Mind you, I have encountered one or two problems whilst in America.

On arrival at Los Angeles airport one year the suitcase of my room-mate went astray.

Everybody else had been cleared at customs and was on his way to the hotel, but being the good pal that I am, I hung about the airport lounge while he desperately searched for his missing case.

I was standing all by myself taking in the scene of this crowded famous airport, wondering if any famous actor or actress would come drifting through, when there was a loud bang!

I didn't really pay much attention to it, as this was followed by another bang!

This second bang was accompanied by frantic, panic-stricken people rushing, running, jumping, diving in all directions of the airport, until I was the only bemused person left standing there.

If any of my former Managers had seen me at that moment it would have confirmed their opinions that I was slow. I just couldn't take it all in as I stood transfixed, simply unable to move. Old ladies with walking sticks whizzed past me and still I didn't move.

Coming from dear old Blighty these things just did not happen; it couldn't possibly have been a gunshot. I looked around quickly to ascertain what all the fuss was about ..... I found out quickly enough as I saw a huge, gargantuous black woman waving a gun about, firing in all directions, a mad crazed look in her non-seeing eyes.

I was only fifteen feet away from her and there were only the two of us in the room, but she was so crazy she didn't see me as she charged about like a huge black enraged bull.

I was now in possession of all my faculties, they were working overtime, as my Blackley instincts for survival searched desperately for an escape route.

I dived head first and lay face down behind my upright suitcase, rolled over onto my back and viewed the position from there ..... It didn't look much better from down there, the situation was grim and all I could see and hear were her huge feet as they flapped about on the tiled floor like a pair of frog-man's flippers.

As I lay there wondering how long it would be before she spotted me, I realised there was another person present in the room. I was horrified to see a little baby sitting quietly upright in its buggy idly playing with its beads.

I couldn't believe it! A quick check revealed the mad woman was at the far end of the room, so I was up onto my knees—a quick, crouched dash out ought to be enough to grab the baby and dash back. It was only when I was in mid-dash in the middle of no man's land that I realised that the child was strapped in. I didn't have time to mess about so I upturned the trolley, baby and all, and dragged the lot back to the sanctuary of my hiding place behind the suitcase, hoping this sudden upset wouldn't set it off crying.

A quick release of the trolley left me and my new companion lying behind the case, which is where we remained for what seemed a lifetime as she continued to shoot at will. My new friend was muttering in my ear, "I don't like the bang! bang!"

"I'm not too keen on it myself," I replied as I patted its back in an attempt to keep it quiet.

Seconds later the automatic airport doors flew open and two Yankee policemen rushed in, guns in hand, crouched positions, and began to circle the room. One of them spotted our unlikely duo on the floor and looked at me with a mixture of anger and astonishment.

"What the hell are you doing here?" he screamed at me.

I didn't really answer; I just looked blankly at him and said "I'm just stuck here"; not really one of the scintillating replies for which I am world famous, but the best I could do under the circumstances.

"Well get the hell out of it," he commanded.

He scared me a bit by his fierceness but not as much as she did with her gun, so I told him, "I don't fancy making a run for it, I'll take my chance lying down here."

When an American policeman tells you to do something he expects you to do it, especially when he's brandishing a gun, and with an "I'm not going to argue with you" he grabbed my leg and, with the baby balanced on my chest, dragged me across the floor towards the door. I moved quite sweetly across the shiny tiled floor, even though my best jacket took a bit of a pounding, but it was a little more difficult as I was bounced across the rubber door mat, along the pavement about 20 yards and left prostrate among the thronging Californian pedestrians, still clutching the baby to my chest.

"Now will you get to hell?" he shouted over his shoulder as he raced back to help his mate to overthrow the lunatic.

He didn't have far to look because she had spotted us leaving the scene and came charging after us.

I felt like the fugitive as I scrambled to my feet, the baby seemed to weigh a ton by this time, and I dashed across the freeway, dodging between huge limousines bearing in on us.

Two strange things happened in my confused mind in the next two minutes. As I dashed away with the baby I was convinced that some do-gooder pedestrian who didn't know what was really going on would think I had snatched a baby and was running away with it, accost me and hand me back over to my friendly policeman.

The other was, as I was crouched down behind the wheel of a parked Greyhound Bus, wondering in which direction to dash next, when I saw the two cops wrestle the mad woman to the ground. In the ensuing struggle, which took quite a while, because she was so strong, her big blond wig rolled from out of the scrimmage and settled in the gutter.

I was convinced that her head had been chopped off; it simply never occurred to me she was wearing a wig as I watched the tussle, gasping for my breath.

As she was finally overpowered and handcuffed, the stark horror of her madness revealed itself.

One passenger reappeared with a bullet in his head, one airport official had two bullets in his arm, one man had been shot in the back. A portable hospital arrived with drips and hospital beds as an emergency unit was set up.

I stood and watched the scene unfold from a short distance

away, still unable to believe it had all actually happened. I didn't realise I still had the baby in my arms until there was a tap on my shoulder and a man said quietly, "That's my son you've got there".

I didn't say a word, just numbly handed the boy over, never to see my 'partner in crime' again.

A couple of weeks later I received a letter from Stephen's parents in Hampshire—I don't know how they found my address—thanking me for my efforts.

This slightly embarrassed me because I knew inwardly that I'd done it all without thinking and I also knew that if I'd have had time to think I wouldn't have done it.

However, I wrote back saying I'm glad Stephen was OK and it was only the normal sort of thing that any super hero would have done!

Meanwhile Georgina Washington, aged 43, was charged with attempted multiple murders. I just hoped they didn't want me to go back for the trial.

One of the highlights of this tour was a trip to Las Vegas.

We had two free days to do what we wanted and Pete Tattersall and I decided to fly to Las Vegas to see the sights.

Peter is part owner of the famous Strawberry Recording Studios, as well as being a successful record producer in his own right, so he is quite used to mixing with top showbusiness stars but even he was not prepared for the events of the next few hours.

We boarded the plane at Los Angeles airport at 10 o'clock in the evening for the 55 minute flight to this gamblers' paradise, this oasis of neon lights and slot machines in the middle of the Nevada Desert.

I was browsing through the 'in flight magazine' when I noticed that Frank Sinatra was appearing at the famous 'Caesar's Palace'. I'm not a fan of Frank Sinatra's but if you are going to Las Vegas then 'Caesar's Palace' with Frank Sinatra is the only place to go. Like those people who never go to football matches, but Liverpool versus Manchester United at Wembley is a must on their social calendar.

I told Peter that this is where we must go that evening, a comment that brought much mirth from the occupant of the other seat in our block.

Apparently tickets had been sold out many months previously and if you didn't have a ticket then you had no chance. Even if you had a ticket it sounded as though you would be lucky to get in.

Undeterred, we decided to go anyway and asked the cab driver to take us straight there without delay because "Ol' blue eyes" was due on stage in 20 minutes.

"Hope you guys have got tickets," the cab driver said to us as we told him our intended destination.

"We didn't even know he was appearing until fifteen minutes ago," we replied.

"You'd be better off staying in the cab with me," he guffawed as he dropped us off outside the imposing entrance of 'Caesars'.

As we entered this 'Palace of Gambling' the scene took my breath away, there were rows upon rows of slot machines standing to attention like military guardsmen, punters playing half a dozen machines at a time, all anxious to give their money away to the establishment.

At the rear of this huge room was the entrance to the theatre.

I marched up to the Maître de oblivious of a thousand eyes watching my every move.

"Excuse me, could you tell me where to get in to see the show?" I enquired politely in my best British accent.

"Have you got your tickets sir?" he replied.

"No!" I said, quite matter of factly.

"Do you see all those people?" he said pointing to a throng of people six deep in a queue that faded out of sight into the distance.

"Well, they all wanna see the show and they ain't got tickets either and they have been here for hours."

I looked at the crowd, looked back at this imposing figure in his immaculately cut uniform and said quietly:

"You are trying to tell me something, aren't you?"

At this he just burst out laughing and said "I like your style, come in," and to the chagrin of the waiting crowd he escorted us into the packed auditorium.

It was a fine sight, jewellery rattling everywhere, pearly teeth flashing on all sides and opulence streaming from all corners.

"Table for two," I said confidently to the flunky who looked at me inquiringly.

"You'll have to share," he said. I feigned a slight look of annoyance at the prospect of sharing, as though it wasn't really what we were used to and agreed, in a most accommodating voice as though I was helping them out of a tricky situation.

"Down the middle, second table on the left," he commanded and we marched down the aisle. Any table in this area was going to be superb, an uninterrupted view, almost as good as being up there with Frank.

Sure enough, two spare seats on the second table on the left; each table seated three and the other seat was already occupied by one of the most famous bald heads in the world. "Sit down, pussycats," he said and we made ourselves comfortable for an evening with 'Kojak'.

Telly Savalas was charm personified as we enjoyed a super performance by 'The Guv'nor' upon the stage.

We hadn't paid to get in, Telly insisted on paying for all our wine and goodies. As well as being one of the best evenings of my life it was also the cheapest!

I was feeling quite euphoric as Frank completed his act, and, quite out of character for me, I announced to Peter that we should complete the evening by meeting the man himself.

His security arrangements and his 'minders' are legend throughout the world, but that never entered my head as I ambled back stage in search of Francis Albert.

Sure enough there he was seated at a table with his wife. Strategically placed on all four sides were four of the biggest gorillas I have ever seen bursting out of their tuxedoes. I decided to approach the one that looked almost human, and he told me that I would have to speak to his famous manager,

Gilly Rizzo, if I wanted to see Francis. He was seated a few feet away just about to tuck into a giant steak. I decided I didn't have time to mess about or bother with any niceties. So I spoke to Gilly in the same manner in which I imagined he spoke to everybody else.

Gilly is a short thick-set, squat man, with a mean face and horn-rimmed glasses who I'm sure had ordered many a dreadful deed to be carried out on anybody who happened to displease him in the past, but I was in the mood for anything as I yelled across to him, "Gilly! I haven't got time to mess about, take us over to Frank because I'm in a rush".

He looked up in amazement, said "Oh! sure, sorry to have kept you," put his knife and fork down, pushed past a few people and hurried over. "Sorry about that," he said. Even I didn't know what was going on now, does he think I'm Prince Charles or something?

"Anybody who's a pal of Joe Louis's is a pal of mine," he said to me as we approached Frank.

Joe Louis, 'The Brown Bomber', former Heavyweight Champion of the world, was now a sick man and worked as a 'greeter' at 'Caeser's', but how he entered the proceedings I'll never know, but I was grateful to him.

"Frank, this guy's from England, a buddy of Joe's," as he pulled out a chair for me to sit down.

I spent an entertaining ten minutes with Frank, hoping Joe Louis wouldn't appear at any moment, sampled his vino, had an interesting chat, and then bade him a fond farewell before my luck ran out.

As I made my way to the exit I saw a huge one-arm bandit, the biggest in the world. I've never gambled on anything in my life, except on myself! but Peter said "With the sort of night you have had, stick a five-dollar piece in". I would have done anything that night ..... the noise was deafening as the jackpot clanged down into the huge bucket at the foot of the machine. I piled all the dollars into my holdall and was off, into the Nevada evening air.

Some people have no luck!

Games in Canada followed, one in the shadow of the amazing Niagara Falls, about 90 miles from Toronto, and another in Kitchener, Ontario, where we played the Canadian National Team. In this game I converted my usual penalty and also collected a lovely 'Man of the Match' Trophy which was not so usual!

The following year our travels took in the lovely Caribbean Islands of Barbados and Tobago, as well as the not so lovely Island of Trinidad.

The games in Barbados were good and well-matched, but my old phrase of "It's not the game, it's the social life that counts" was never more apparent than on this trip.

I've always prided myself as being a good pro' and with me 'the game' always comes first, but the island is so beautiful and so unspoilt, the beaches so white and inviting, the pace of life so leisurely and uncomplicated that it was easy to slip into the rhythm of things there.

I am also a virtual non-drinker, but must admit I enjoyed one or two rum punches as I sampled the delights of the island.

One of the 'delights' of the island I had no intention of sampling, however, were the attentions outside our hotel of a rather effeminate 'gentleman' who sported a pink suit, pink silk cravat, white crocodile shoes and a pink handbag to complete his ensemble.

Each time a group of us left the hotel he would look at me and hiss through his teeth, much to the merriment of my colleagues. I didn't take too kindly to my special treatment but decided that if I ignored him he would go away, but this continued day after day.

One night after a game, the whole team had gone out together to a night club to celebrate yet another defeat! and being the elder statesman of the team ..... by far, I decided at 2 am that it was time for me to hit the sack so I left the lads to it, knowing it would be dawn before they made their way back.

I was walking back to our hotel, all alone, miles from anywhere, in a strange country, at two in the morning, I really should have known better, but all I could think of was my bed and a good night's sleep.

From out of the bushes I heard psst,! psst,! I recognised the sound immediately and suddenly I felt wide awake again as the pink suit emerged from the shrubs, the handbag hanging limply from his wrist.

I decided attack was the best form of defence, one of the features about these tropical islands is that there always seems to be branches from trees lying everywhere in the road. When you are driving around you hit them constantly and I have often cursed their presence, but not on this occasion as I picked up the biggest, held it like a cudgel and whilst trying to adopt the most aggressive tone possible in my voice, informed him that if he took one more step forward I was going to bury it into his skull.

His big eyes rolled like billiard balls as he told me he just wanted to be my friend.

The look on my face must have been enough to provide the answer because he turned on his heels and fled.

Two nights later we had attended a reception at The Hilton Hotel, way over on the opposite side of the island to our hotel, and at 3 am, Bobby Smith, by this time Manager of Swindon Town, Geoff Priestner and myself were happily returning to our hotel, after a thoroughly entertaining evening. I was driving our hired moke, a mixture of a mini and a jeep, when in the middle of nowhere the damn thing broke down, there was nothing for it but to get out and push; I never realised they had hills in Barbados!

We took it in turns, one to steer, two of us to push. We were in this situation on a particularly barren stretch of road, Geoff Priestner steering, Bob and I almost horizontal, as we pushed the moke up the incline, sweat was streaming off us as we gave maximum effort, muscles taut, backs bent, two big bottoms stuck up in the air as we pushed and pushed ..... then a familiar sound hit my ears, psst! psst! psst! I knew it wasn't a snake in the bushes as Bob and I looked at each other in our very un-gentlemanly positions, a quick look towards the bushes and there he was, pink suit neatly pressed, his pink handbag glittering in the moonlight.

Without a single word, Geoff put on the handbrake, Bob and I walked around to the front of the vehicle, and we both then proceeded to **drag** it up the hill ..... it's better to be safe than sorry!

It seems that Geoff, Bob and I are fated where transport is concerned; when we moved on to Trinidad we had a similar bad experience.

Trinidad was, without doubt the biggest disappointment to me of all the 30-odd countries I have visited.

Whenever I have read reports of test matches between England and The West Indies in Port of Spain I have always imagined it to be a beautiful island, palm trees, rolling seas, white beaches, happy smiling coloured kids, glowing with health and vitality, their skins shining as a result of their vigorous outdoor life ..... I was wrong.

I found a cosmopolitan island with almost every nationality represented, mostly Indians and Pakistanis. I didn't see any palm trees, the roads were filthy, the air polluted. I searched but didn't find a beach. The faces of the people, not the true Trinidad people, but I didn't see many of them, were dull, lifeless, suspicious and unsmiling and the kids certainly did not glow with health and vitality, all in all a thoroughly depressing and miserable place.

The highlight of the social side of the trip was an audience with the British High Commissioner at his private residence, attended by all his Ministers.

It was a delightful, informal gathering as the Minister for Sport, Minister of Transport etc, mingled with us and made us feel at home.

We were all on our best behaviour, all anxious to observe the correct protocol, say all the correct things, use the correct knives and crook our little fingers when we had coffee. 'Brooky' set us on the right path when he was asked if he would like a prawn cocktail and he quite rightly replied "No, thank you, I'll have a drink with my meal"! It's on occasions like these that 'Brooky' is at his best and we are only too happy to follow his example.

When given the menu to study he informed the rest of us that MINUTE steaks were the order of the day, so politely informed the waiter that if they were so small that they were described as minute, then we would all have two each!

He's really valuable at times like these.

We played two games in Trinidad, a great game against the Champions in Port of Spain and one in the middle of the jungle, somewhere in the centre of the island.

Taxis were allocated to drive us there and as Bob, Geoff and I boarded ours, joined by 'Brooky' and Wally Roberts, I predicted that if this taxi got us there it certainly would not get us back.

How right I was, we just managed to arrive in one piece after hitting two goats who were quietly chewing grass, tethered to a post outside a house. The driver corrected the vehicle, pointed it back in the right direction and careered off down the road. We also hit a few hens which had the nerve to cross in front of us as we sallied forth and it was with great relief that I stumbled out of the cab when we finallay got to the ground.

My back ached with the bumping and I was feeling less like playing a match than ever before.

At the end of the game, I tried to muscle into a different taxi but without any success and we were all stuck with the same madman as before.

I just instinctively knew it wouldn't get us back to Port of Spain but there was nothing else for it but to hop in and hope for the best.

One o'clock in the morning, after a hard game of football, to be lying on a dirt track road in the middle of Trinidad is not to be recommended and is not featured in any of the Thomsons Holiday Brochures.

The driver had his head under the bonnet of his taxi tinkering and cursing as we lay in the dust trying to go to sleep.

This was no problem for 'Brooky', who can sleep on the

proverbial clothes line; I have often seen him go to sleep during football matches that he has been playing in! and soon there were the familiar Zs coming from his nose. "A man who sleeps well has few worries." Well, if that is the case then 'Brooky' hasn't got a care in the world as we all lay there watching him twitch.

In the distance we saw two searchlights pierce the sky, they came nearer and nearer and we all spread ourselves across the road, except 'Brooky' who was still asleep; if the driver didn't stop he would knock us all down, even that wouldn't have surprised me.

The vehicle ground to a halt in front of us. We resembled a picket line at Grunwicks and we begged a lift back to Port of Spain.

The driver told us to jump into the back of his open truck.

His truck was a battered old pig van, used for transporting pigs, livestock, and pigswill across Trinidad. "What about the smell," Bob said as we jumped aboard. "Too bad"! I replied, "the pigs will just have to get used to it"! as we tried to shake 'Brooky' back to life.

We all gratefully clambered aboard leaving our poor taxi driver still tinkering under his bonnet as we tried to get a grip on something as we rolled about in the back of the truck.

I've always wanted to ride into town on an open-top vehicle waving to the crowds, but I didn't expect to do it in Trinidad with half a dozen pigs and Brooky to keep me company.

Another success from the penalty spot against the National Team in Dar-Es-Salaam by my good self is my fondest memory of Tanzania but Kenya was quite frankly another disappointment.

I thought the food was appalling, the hygiene left a lot to be desired and due to a military coup in Nairobi we had to stay for sixteen days.

As a special treat we were taken to a Masai village where a warrior in full traditional regalia ..... complete with Adidas trainers with no laces!! pointed to his hut and told us proudly that it was made from Wildebeest 'droppings' ..... the way we felt, our squad could have built them a new town hall!!!

twenty-nine

"A MAN OF PROPERTY"

Back home, I thought my 'career' was winding down and deliberately signed to play in a lower league than I had been used to, to simply enjoy a final fling, help any player in the team who appreciated a bit of help and to generally enjoy my game, giving it everything I'd got for the 90 minutes of course but with no real pressures.

I signed for the famous amateur side Northern Nomads where 'Brooky' had played for fifteen years man and beast! expecting to renew my full-back partnership with him.

This I did, but only after a scare from the Manager, Doug Walker, an ex-Manchester City goalkeeping colleague of mine. He told me before the season started:

"Yes! come along for training and we'll try and sort something out for you." 'Brooky' was standing with me at the time and as Doug drove off in his car I said:

"God, it must be some team you've got here, if he only **might** sort something out for me," and sure enough I only made an appearance as a substitute in the first pre-season friendly game. That was enough, however, to prove to Doug that I was up to the required standard and I was never left out of the team the whole time I was there, but in a way I even had to have a bloody trial to sign for Northern Nomads!

Doug Walker is a great man and was a huge asset to Northern Nomads and I really enjoyed playing for him. I had a super time as a 'Nomad'. With my past record it was fitting that I signed for them at some time!

Doug, however, is also a very intelligent and successful businessman and his work was encroaching into his football. I could tell he was going to resign, so when I received an offer from another ex-colleague, David Wild, to sign for Chadderton I did so and 'Brooky' came along with me.

If I thought Doug Walker would have stayed as Manager I would have stayed with him, but I was sure he was going and he did in fact retire shortly afterwards.

It was 'interesting' to say the least at Chadderton. There were times when David wasn't at the games, through illness, working and scouting, and on these occasions I was put in charge of the team as a player/manager. Being a player/manager is one of the hardest jobs in the world. It's not easy to be standing, shivering, in your muddy kit at half-time, attempting to put right the problems of the first half when inwardly you know that you, yourself were one of the major problems.

However, I felt comfortable in the role. I spoke to each player in turn, told him what I thought his failings were, told him what I thought his strengths were and that we were all going to play to each other's strengths and play around the weaknesses.

The response on each occasion from the players was tremendous, even renowned troublesome players were never any trouble with me. David was always appreciative of my efforts and used to discuss everything with me ..... except the time he decided to leave me out of the team.

It was a freezing cold day, but it was lovely and warm in my car so I decided to go in my shirt sleeves to the match. Two strides from the car to the warm dressing-room was all I would be subjected to the cold, so I would be OK.

As I arrived I thought David gave me a rather sheepish look but didn't pay much attention to it as I entered the dressing-room.

He then gave me the usual immortal words "You've been playing well but I want to see how the younger players do with a view to next season". "OK," I replied, but I said I couldn't stay and watch the game even though I wanted to because I was only in my shirt sleeves and it was so cold I had just seen a brass monkey with a blow lamp looking for a welder!

He said he understood and I drove away from the ground, little knowing I would never return.

The following day I received a call from Wigan Athletic. Harry McNally, the Manager from my Chorley days, was now the Manager of the reserve team at Wigan.

They were a young side and needed an old head (is there an older one) like mine to help them along. Would I like to join them?

It was a great move for me. Wigan Athletic were the cream of non-league football. Their ground, Springfield Park, is superior to many league grounds, and compared to the slag heaps I had been playing on recently it seemed like Wembley to me. The job Harry wanted me to do also really appealed, but even though I felt a little hard done to the day before, I still felt a little bit of loyalty towards David Wild.

Harry wanted me to play on Tuesday evening and I said I would let him know after telephoning David Wild to put him in the picture and discuss the situation.

I didn't have to telephone David, however, because later that day he rang me.

"Do you want to play in the reserves on Tuesday?" he said. Chadderton Reserves versus Irlam Town Reserves was not a fixture that really gripped my imagination but, being a good pro', always wanting to set a good example and to let everybody know that Fred Eyre is not too big time to accept being relegated to the reserve team, I would, under normal circumstances, have been prepared to play.

The FA Rules state that a player can play in both of the two totally unconnected leagues that Chadderton and Wigan Athletic Reserves play in without transferring the player's registration, so I could play for both teams without any fuss.

So I said to David "If it's the reserve team I'd rather not ..... I was going to go on and tell him about Wigan Athletic and how flattered I was that they had showed interest in an old lag like me and could I, if he did not object, go over and see them on Tuesday evening instead. But he simply slammed the 'phone down in mid-sentence and that was the end of my spell at Chaddy!!

With this small question of my loyalty to him now apparently answered, I drove over to Wigan to enter yet another interesting phase of my life.

I arrived at Springfield Park, as with all my other matches, in very good time, swung the gleaming Rolls into the car park, but did not get out.

All of a sudden I got a feeling that I had never had before ..... I felt very old. I simply could not bring myself to enter the ground, I just sat in the car and listened to the radio.

Soon, young kids began to arrive, clutching Tesco bags which presumably contained their boots. Each lad seemed to be dressed the same, faded jeans, Adidas training shoes, donkey jacket. We laugh at the Chinese all being dressed the same, but we are not much better ourselves!

I heard one young player remark "The referee must be worth a few bob," as he pointed to me and the car.

Little did he know that in half an hour he would be lining up alongside me.

Still I didn't move. I just didn't want to go through the door. Here I was, successful businessman, veteran of 1,000 games, who'd travelled the world, and I was reticent about going into the dressing-room at Wigan Athletic.

Eventually I could leave it no longer. As with all match days, I was dressed in a smart suit, shirt and tie, just the opposite to my team mates. As the opposition coach arrived at the ground, I walked in with them, but when we got through the door, they all turned right and I turned left into the door marked Home Team.

What a performance, just to enter the ground; little did I know a couple of years later I would be appointed Manager of the Club.

As with my days at Chorley, I loved playing for Harry

McNally. His ideas on how the game should be played coincided with mine, the players I rate highly, so does he, and we both can spot 'a donkey' a hundred miles away.

I was having an Indian Summer, and I wanted it to last for ever. I gained the respect of the kids, they did what I asked and I carried Harry's instructions out onto the field to the letter. Life was dealing me a good hand to finish off my career.

We reached a Cup Final, only to lose to Accrington Stanley, the only Cup Final I ever lost in my life, but I was grateful to even have been there at my stage of life, and as I looked round the dressing-room at the end and saw a few tears being shed, I knew we had given everything we had, and I felt I had contributed quite a bit myself.

Football, however, has a way of knocking the legs from under you, and two weeks later the directors of Wigan Athletic Football Club announced that they were disbanding their Reserve Team 'for financial reasons', so a host of talented young players were released. Harry McNally was out of a job and I was out to grass; should I finally call it a day and concentrate on my business?

Business, thankfully, continued to prosper; the shop, the plum site on Princess Street, was doing well and I thought I was set there for life ..... until a tall distinguished-looking gentleman came into the shop one lunchtime.

I was in the shop at the time as he walked through the door, ignored the counter, which is where most customers head for, looked round the whole shop, up into the corners, his eyes missing nothing as he surveyed the entire scene!

I stood and watched him, quietly amused at this unusual situation.

I became slightly less amused as he wandered down to our private quarters at the rear of the shop, still casting a professional eye over every little thing.

"Can I help you?" I enquired trying desperately to conceal my anger.

"No! it's all right," he replied casually still eyeing up the place.

"I'm afraid it's not all right," I corrected him. "I own this shop and this department is not accessible to the public."

"My clients are contemplating buying this building and I need to inform them what they are getting for their money."

At this point two things happened. Firstly I slung the man out of the shop and secondly I decided there and then to move.

I have always tried to be decisive but I was at my best on this occasion. I arrived home that evening and as I tucked into my evening meal, I informed Judith, quite matter of factly, that Fred Eyre Stationers would be moving.

"Where to?" was her obvious first question and I had to admit that I hadn't a clue, but we would definitely be moving, and furthermore, when we did move I would own the building this time. There would never be an occasion again when a total stranger would walk through the door and announce a change of landlord. From this day on I would be my own landlord. I don't know who the gentleman was but his visit that day did me the biggest favour possible, it made me think of something that had simply never entered my head before, buy my own building ..... become a man of property.

As in the past, years previously, I thought Sunday would be the best day to begin my search and I went through the same ritual as I had before in search of premises, only this time my sights were set a little higher.

Eventually, after much searching, my mind kept coming back to a building on John Dalton Street, a quality business street about 50 yards from my present position.

It looked an ideal building with six floors, including a shop, ample office space and plenty of much needed storage space for stock. I thought it would suit my purposes admirably. The only problem was that it wasn't for sale.

The shop was 'To Let' and so were each of the individual offices, but I thought it was expecting a lot for each unit to be let individually so I decided to jump straight in and offer a price to buy the lot.

It was a pretty bold step for a Blackley boy to take. It meant a few hardships. Our holiday house, bought in conjunction with

'Brooky' as an investment in Anglesey, had to be sold, a bit of belt tightening here and there, but nothing too drastic. The lovely house I had bought my parents near to us in Worsley had been paid for in full, I owned every brick of that, so that was no problem. It is one of my greatest thrills to see them so nicely settled in a house of their own with no worries, so I wouldn't do anything to jeopardise that. No! I think I can just about afford the building, and anyway I can always get a paper round in my spare time!

I managed to clinch the deal and a matter of weeks later I became the owner of a complete six-storey building in the City Centre of Manchester. I then set about refurbishing the place to my own specification and as with my previous premises there were only three people left there at 3 am as we locked up, my preparations complete for the big opening six hours later. As in the past my Mother and Father had stayed the course with me until the last nail was knocked in.

My move to John Dalton Street proved to be a wise one, from the start. It is a very prestigious position and the passing trade is much, much greater. Also I now don't have the minor irritation of having to pay rent every month!

Harry McNally, meanwhile, had been appointed Assistant Manager at Southport Football Club in the Fourth Division of the Football League.

Southport had been struggling for many seasons and often had to apply for re-election to the league at the end of the season.

Now they had appointed a new management team of Hughie Fisher as player-manager and Harry McNally as his assistant.

I thought this a sensible appointment because Hughie Fisher had been and indeed still was a very good player. Having begun his career at Blackpool he moved on to Southampton, where he held down a first team place for many seasons, and indeed was substitute in the 1976 Cup Final when Southampton surprisingly beat Manchester United 1-0 at Wembley with a goal from little Bobby Stokes.

Now he felt ready to move into management, but having

dealt with the level of player that was out of the reach of Southport, it was felt he needed the assistance of a man who knew the lower regions of the game inside out. Such a man was Harry McNally.

Harry proved his shrewdness again by signing me for Southport! So at an age when most players are thinking of taking up tiddleywinks or chess I found myself back with a Football League Club again.

He wanted me to do the same job again with the kids, and of course I was happy to do it.

I was also to receive some remuneration for my efforts, but having driven an 80-mile round trip every Tuesday evening and Thursday evening plus the same trip for the game on a Saturday the £1.50 I received for the entire week didn't really stretch to much high living! Thank goodness I didn't have to pay tax on it!

However, it mattered little to me because I was embarking on another very happy period. I loved my time at Southport and was extremely sad as I entered the TV room of our hotel in Cornwall 'Bedruthan Steps' where I go with my family every year. I switched on just in time to hear that Southport Football Club had at last lost its league status and their place in the Football Legaue was to be taken by Wigan Athletic.

This short, simple statement meant nothing to me at that moment, only sorrow at Southport's plight, but it was to be a very significant moment for me as far as my football career was concerned.

thirty

WIGAN ATHLETIC FOOTBALL CLUB

Wigan Athletic's acceptance into The Football League, after many unsuccessful applications, meant a complete reappraisal of everything at Springfield Park.

Firstly, all concerned had to change from part-time to full-time. The Manager, The Secretary, The Groundsman and, of course, the players.

This was not as easy and straightforward as it sounds. Many players had reached a stage in their jobs where they were simply too old to change their occupations. They were good enough to play in the Fourth Division, but having attained a certain level in their working lives, felt it unwise for them to throw it all away for the 'glamour' of being a full-time professional footballer for a couple of seasons.

Also it was felt that the now defunct Reserve Team should be resurrected and with this in mind, keeper Phil Critchley suggested to Manager Ian McNiell that I would be ideal for the job of running the Reserve team.

I always knew Phil was a good goalkeeper, but hadn't realised that he possessed such perception and also it says much for Mr McNiell that he felt confident enough to give me the chance.

I accepted the job, never mentioning whether or not I was to be paid. I also asked for and was given 'Brooky' as my right-hand man, even though Mr McNiell had other, more experienced, pros in mind for the job and this was the first instance where Ian McNiell showed his qualities as a leader by giving me the job, giving me the man I wanted alongside me and from that moment on never interfering with the way I tackled the job.

I like to think, of course, that I never gave him any cause to worry. I'm sure if I had done anything to displease him he would have straightened me out, but the fact remained that he left me completely alone to do the job, and I presume, in view of the fact that he never interfered, that I must have done it to his satisfaction.

I know that we were extremely pleased to have him as our Boss. Both 'Brooky' and I had the utmost respect for him, we thought and still think that he is a fine man, a super person, who always stood by us, and did a great job for Wigan Athletic whilst he was the Manager. It was indeed a sad day in the Eyre and Brooks households when two and a half seasons later we learned that he was to lose his job.

Our brief, quite simply, at the outset was to get a team onto the field for the first game against Blackpool. The Boss had problems of his own, about eight weeks to turn the whole club into a full-time set up. We had about four weeks to sift through the many trialists to find a team from scratch to compete at the same level as the youngsters of Manchester United, City, Liverpool, Everton and the rest.

I set myself a list of rules that I intended to follow the whole time I was in Football Management at whatever level it might be and up to now I have found no cause to stray from them.

I have encountered so many bad Managers and Coaches during my career, that if I treat my players in exactly the opposite way that most of them treated me, then I knew I would be on the right lines! Be honest, I can't see any reason for telling lies to players.

Be organised. Know exactly what you are going to do in training, know exactly what you want in matches and know exactly what you are going to say when certain situations crop up.

This, together with my basic knowledge of the game, my memory for players from yesteryear and from the present day has stood me in good stead in dealing with players of all ages and temperaments.

My favourite species in football is 'The Good Pro'. There is nothing I admire more in soccer than a good professional. Since taking charge of the Reserve team at Wigan it has been a pleasure to team up with some for whom I hold a very high regard.

I was perhaps fortunate in that the first of these was Micky Worswick, a tremendous favourite with the Springfield Park fans for many years. Micky was in the Wigan Athletic team when it was elected to the league but felt he was a little too old to turn full-time.

His attitude and application set the trend for the rest of the players and not one of them has ever let me down, despite the obvious disappointment of not being in the first team where they felt they belonged.

All the players I have handled have been a credit to themselves and their profession and in fact in the three seasons I have been at Wigan I have never had to deal with any grizzly pros. This is a good job because I feel that this type of player is a cancer to the game, and should be removed as quickly as possible, and if I ever encounter any of them they will be through the door in double quick time before they spread their bad habits to the other players.

From the minute I arrived at Springfield Park as a coach, I felt completely at home. I really loved the place, a feeling I had not really known since my days at Maine Road. I felt it a little at Chorley, a little at Rossendale, both nice homely clubs, but I had a special feeling at Springfield Park.

The main reason of course was the Manager, but the Secretary, Derek Welsby, also went out of his way to help me and make me feel at home.

Ronnie Pye made life easier for me on training nights, regarding the facilities available. The Chairman and Directors were polite and treated me as a member of the staff, which of course I now was, but I was only part-time after all, and even though Brooky and I were constantly aware of this, it seemed to make no difference to the Directors who treated us with respect.

In fact everybody was really kind ..... except for the door-man.

This gentleman, who manned the Main Entrance on match days, really put 'Brooky' and I in our place when we arrived for the first home game of the season.

We both arrived together, and parked our beautiful cars in the deserted car park, because as usual we had arrived extra early. The sun was shining as we strolled together towards the official players' entrance, both thinking how smart we looked in our best suits, shirts and ties, everything that two smart young coaches should be wearing on match days.

"Good afternoon," we greeted the steward cheerfully as we side-stepped him to go through the narrow door.

"You can't come in here," he growled, as he moved across to completely block the door.

"Why not?" we enquired, trying not to look too put out.

"The caterers go in through the entrance further down," was his reply which really took the wind out of our sails.

"Do we look like the men who deliver the pies?"

Still, this was only a minor irritation and nothing, not even the steward, could dampen our spirits as we set to work for our new Club.

The first season in the Football League was a huge success for Wigan Athletic. They finished a highly respectable sixth in the league, and my reserve side finished a little higher in our league, so it was a good season for both teams. This was rewarded by the Directors with a fortnight's holiday in Majorca, a gesture which was really appreciated by all the players and even more so by 'Brooky' and myself, who were also invited along at the insistence of Mr McNiell. The Directors originally suggested a round the world cruise, but the players wanted to go somewhere else!

The second season things went even better, the first team

finished in sixth place again and my team ended up even higher than it did the previous season.

This was coupled with a good cup run when we disposed of Blackpool and Northwich Victoria, both after replays, and a memorable victory at Stamford Bridge when a Tommy Gore chip was enough to eliminate the famous Chelsea 1-0 and put Wigan into the hat for a tremendous fixture away at Everton.

Goodison Park was crammed with 52,000 people, the biggest gate of the season. About 20,000 were from Wigan all hoping to see 'Latics perform one of the biggest giant-killing acts of all time.

Unfortunately they were to be disappointed, not in the performance of the team, but in the result. Goals from Joe McBride, Brian Kidd and Bob Latchford gave the Toffeemen a 3-0 victory, but this still did nothing to diminish another fine season, and again the directors sent us off on holiday, this time to sunny Malta for a week's rest at the top hotel on the island.

Trips abroad like this, continual ground improvements, good performances on the field, a youth policy that was paying dividends in unearthing, developing and producing its own young players, first-class travel to games, best hotel accommodation, all of these things went together to make people inside football sit up and take notice. Here was a football club that did things in the correct manner, a club that was going places, a club of substance and above all a club with great potential.

This potential was recognised by the shrewd eye of Mr Freddie Pye, Chairman of Stockport County, who I feel must have looked at the set up at Springfield Park, and compared it to his own at Edgeley Park. His shrewd eye became an envious one.

Although comparative infants to League Football, the difference between the two clubs is vast and Mr Pye saw more scope to achieve his ambition of being Chairman of a successful Football Club at Wigan than there was at Stockport County.

Freddie Pye is a self-made man, a Stockport lad who wanted to be a professional footballer and who, like myself, never quite made the top grade, but graced the lower regions, playing for a number of clubs in the Cheshire League and the Welsh League.

This story sounds a little familiar!

He then thought that if he was going to end up on the scrap-heap at least he would own it! and indeed opened a number of scrap metal yards in and around the Manchester area, and secured his business future. At the same time he was the successful Manager of Altrincham, when, under his guidance plus the drive and enthusiasm of present chairman Noel White and the former chairman Peter Swales, now of course Chairman of Manchester City, they put the hitherto unknown name of Altrincham Football Club on the map.

So with his business acumen and his association with soccer, both as a player and a Manager, he brought a little more knowledge to the position of Chairman than one would normally expect.

Mr Pye also has a reputation of always getting what he wants and he decided he wanted to join the board of Wigan Athletic ... so he joined the board of Wigan Athletic ..... he then decided he wanted to be Chairman of Wigan Athletic ..... so he became Chairman of Wigan Athletic.

The present Chairman, Mr Horrocks, became President of the club, a move which pleased me personally because I always felt that Mr Horrocks added a touch of dignity to the club, was proud to be part of Wigan Athletic and was a fine ambassador for the club.

Mr Pye's first move was to invite on to the board England's number one footballer for many years, the incomparable Bobby Charlton. His 106 caps, his never-to-be-forgotten goals, his impeccable behaviour on the field for Manchester United and England, made him a legend throughout the world and now here he was with me at Wigan Athletic ..... two living legends together!

As far as 'Brooky' and I were concerned the first bombshell of the new season came when Mr McNiell informed us that the club intended to withdraw us from The Lancashire League, the league that had served us so well the previous two seasons and enter us in the newly formed Umbro Floodlight League.

This brought about my first ever conflict with the Manager. The Umbro League operated only in midweek, which meant that except for the players on first team duty the whole of the Wigan Athletic playing staff was redundant every Saturday, traditionally the footballing day of the week.

Entering a midweek league almost completely cancelled out the midweek training sessions for the non-contract players whom I was responsible for, so the young players, whom the club was relying on for its future, were to receive neither coaching nor fitness training.

If all of this wasn't bad enough, the league consisted of five other teams. How anybody could contemplate even forming a league containing only six teams is beyond my comprehension, and when I was informed that we were to be one of the big six I simply couldn't understand the reasoning behind it.

Some other teams, I discovered, had remained in their various other leagues and were using this 'Umbro' league as an auxiliary league, so increasing their number of games, but we were to be solely represented in this little league.

I could only assume that the Boss was not in possession of all the facts, so 'Brooky' and I each took a morning off work to enlighten him, and we were confident that we could change his mind ..... we were wrong. 'The Umbro Floodlight League' it was to be.

My first thought and my second and third was to resign my position at the club.

This was something that I was loath to do really, but this simple, stubborn decision to me spelled disaster with a capital 'D'. The continuity of young players, which always takes a couple of years to get rolling, would now be broken and I knew it would be difficult to pick up the threads.

I wouldn't be able to train and coach the players, which was something I felt I had proved I could do successfully, and I felt that their progress would be hampered by the lack of attention, so taking things all round I felt that there really wasn't a job left for me to do.

It was only Dave Brooks's insistence that "I gave it a go" for the season that kept me at Wigan Athletic. "Maybe The Boss will realise his mistake by the end of the season."

It gives me no pleasure to recall that he admitted to a severe error of judgement a long time before the season ended. By this time unfortunately the damage had already been done. As far as I am concerned the Reserve team set up, so good and professional and well organised in the past, simply spluttered along and eventually ground to a halt when we didn't play a single game for over two months. I felt it was all so unnecessary and self-destructive that during this period I confided in Dave Brooks that I definitely intended to "jack the job in". Again he dissuaded me. "Wait a few more weeks, and then tell The Boss that if we remain in this league next year we will be leaving," he suggested. I agreed but didn't realise that many unlikely happenings would take place during those "few more weeks".

There had been rumblings of discontent amongst the spectators for a number of weeks, as they watched the 'Latics stumble from game to game.

They made it quite clear that they, the paying public, were far from satisfied with the team's performances this season.

After the relative successes of the previous two seasons, they had hoped for something more in 1981 and when it became apparent that they were not going to get what they wanted, they singled out Ian McNiell for the treatment that is fast becoming part and parcel of a Manager's job.

A little bit of barracking here and there on the terraces, one or two significant little asides in the newspapers, a few letters to the club, people sidling up to me in the town with knowing looks on their faces, each one forecasting the impending departure of 'The Boss'. Whenever this occurred I always made my feelings quite clear, we worked for him and we supported him but the occasions when 'Brooky' would appear and remove me from the 'ear bashings' I was receiving from 'Latics fans were becoming more and more frequent.

It got so bad that I abandoned my usual practice of nipping

into the Social Club for a drink after matches and chose instead to go straight home, rather than get involved in arguments supporting Ian McNiell. I could see, however, that the team was not responding on the field and after viewing an abysmal performance away to Port Vale, that we lost three nil (to be honest we were lucky to get nil and they were unlucky not to get eight or nine) I remarked to my Dad as we sadly left the ground, "I don't think The Boss will survive this one," and unfortunately I was correct.

Monday 16th February was just like any other Monday at Fred Eyre Stationers until Freddie Pye rang and asked me to go and see him at his office.

The thoughts in my mind as I drove to his office near Plymouth Grove were that The Boss had been sacked, together with Kenny Banks and Ian Gillibrand, his two right hand men at the club, and that they were dispensing with the entire staff, a clean sweep and that 'Brooky' and I were to go along with them.

"Thanks for everything in the past, please inform your mate 'Brooky'," and that would be that ..... Thank you and goodnight! Goodnight Vienna! Still we had done our best, until we were whipped out of the Lancashire League ..... they are probably right, there isn't really a job for us to do now ..... and I was so fed up with the situation I was going to pack the job in anyway so I can't really blame them.

"Mr Eyre to see you Mr Pye," said his secretary into the intercom.

I entered the Chairman's large office, admired the many photographs of Fred with Members of the Royal Family, Fred with some of the world's top sportsmen, but none of Fred with Frank Sinatra ..... he's got a long way to go!

I sat down and prepared myself for the news. I knew inwardly that he was going to tell me he had sacked The Boss, but I wasn't really prepared for what came next.

"We would like you to take over as Manager of Wigan Athletic until we appoint a new man," he said.

It came as a shock to me, I didn't want to be the Manager of a football club and I remembered I hadn't enjoyed my last experience in this position.

I suggested that if it was only to be until a new man was found, then why not say nothing to Mr McNiell and let him carry on until they found somebody, secretly hoping that if this were to happen, the team might start winning again and the crisis would be forgotten and Mr McNiell would never have known that there had been a problem and he would have kept his job. This suggestion was knocked back. It was felt that a change was necessary.

"What about 'Banksie' or 'Gilly', they are full-time and could keep things ticking over?" This was rejected out of hand, there was only me left, so after accepting the fact that there was nothing I could do to keep Mr McNiell in the job, I said that I would become Manager of Wigan Athletic. I asked for Brooky again to be my assistant and when I approached him later in the day, he readily agreed but stressed he couldn't start immediately, unlike me, because he had to rearrange all his appointments, but would start as my right hand man in about ten days' time.

My first day in charge gave me relatively few problems, the main one was in my own house. My son Steven, a staunch Ian McNiell fan, was so upset at the thought of him losing his job that I couldn't get him off to school.

Seeing Ian McNiell at the ground was also a bit of a tear jerker for me, but a brief chat with him, a quick talk with the players and a good light-hearted training session with them soon lifted the air of depression which hung over Springfield Park.

I decided not to make changes in the team simply for the sake of making them, but thought there was no point in selecting the same line up as before, because something was obviously wrong, or Mr McNiell would still be in charge, so I decided to do the job, for whatever length of time, my own way, pick my own team, what I considered the best on the day, and stand or fall by my own decisions, which is really all I have ever done.

The computer had thrown us a particularly hard fixture for

my first game as a Manager, we were to play high flying Mansfield Town at Springfield Park.

'The Stags' were placed third in the league, and although looking a good bet for promotion, couldn't afford to drop any points because there were a number of teams on their tail.

I decided to be bold and decisive and made seven changes from the squad who performed so badly the previous week at Port Vale. I was obviously hoping for a win, but an improvement in attitude, application, will to win, a desire to help each other during the game, a neatness and smartness in appearance when attending the game, a little thing that I felt had been sadly lacking, was what I asked for and was exactly what I received from the players.

As I watched them leave the dressing-room I knew that if we were to lose this match it would only be because Mansfield were a great team and had beaten us by playing super football. I knew that if we were to lose it would not be for lack of effort.

The crowd were understandably a little subdued at first, obviously wondering what this new unknown Manager would be serving up for them, but when they saw the quality of football the players produced and the amount of honest sweat and toil they put in, they got right behind us and cheered us all the way to a wonderful 2-0 victory.

There is nothing to this Manager's job ..... all you have to do is win matches!

The following week moved along just as sweetly as the first, varied training sessions, something different each day helped to keep the players alert and keen, a new voice, fresh, bright, new ideas, a new approach helped them enjoy their training and soon Saturday was upon us again.

Another plum fixture, Bury away at Gigg Lane, a local Derby. Our performance last week should ensure a good following for the short trip across Lancashire plus the opportunity to see the 'Latics' former favourite Tommy Gore, my room mate on the Malta and Majorcan jaunts, in action for his new club, having been transferred from Wigan earlier in the season following a number of little disagreements with Ian McNiell.

All in all the stage was set for a good afternoon as our coach weaved its way through the cobbled streets of Bury, about ten minutes away from Gigg Lane. It was a fairly quiet scene as players read the newspaper, others played cards, some idly gazed out of the window at the shoppers in the busy Lancashire streets, some of them wearing Bury colours as they made their way to the ground.

"Put the radio on driver, let's have a bit of music," came a voice from the back of the coach.

The driver clicked the switch, and as if by remote control the announcer's voice blared out "Wigan Athletic have just announced that Nottingham Forest and England Centre Half, Larry Lloyd, has been appointed their player-manager, he will commence his duties during the middle of next week." I have never seen such looks of amazement on so many faces at one time, it seemed an eternity before anybody spoke.

I must admit, I was as shocked as the players. I naively thought, I might have been given the word before the media so as not to be caught on the hop. It didn't upset me at all, because I knew I was only filling in until a new appointment was made, but, on the team bus radio, five minutes before reaching the ground prior to an important fixture was ill-timed to say the least.

Still, we were stuck with the situation now and it was my job to get the minds of the players back on the job in hand, to beat Bury in three-quarters of an hour's time.

I pulled out all my old scripts to try and brighten up the dressing-room; if only Brooky was with me we could have performed our double act, but I was on my own. In fact by the time he was ready to take up his appointment as my assistant, the job had gone ..... it was all over ..... so he nearly became an Assistant Manager.

A battery of photographers were at the players' tunnel as my team took the field, but unfortunately the lenses were not directed at them but at the Directors' box, where Larry Lloyd was seated, having a preliminary look at the team that he was to inherit the following week. I hoped he wasn't going to be disappointed.

Again the players did not let me, or themselves, down and played with tremendous spirit and skill and I felt their performance warranted a little more than a 0-0 draw.

So I was ready to hand over to Larry Lloyd with a record that should ensure me a place in the 'Guinness Book of Records' as the only Football League Manager never to lose a game, never to concede a goal in his entire management career ..... and still lose his job!

I was, however, hoping for a small consolation of half a bottle of whisky by being named 'Bell's Manager of the Fortnight'!

Larry Lloyd has enjoyed a glittering career. Born in Bristol, he stands 6ft 2in and looks a commanding figure at the heart of any defence.

He began his career with Bristol Rovers, played 43 games for them before being snapped up by Liverpool in a £50,000 deal.

During his 150-game reign at Anfield he earned England Under 23 honours and in 1971 gained his first full international cap. He then moved on to Coventry City for £250,000 and played another 50 games at Highfield Road before signing for Nottingham Forest for a bargain £60,000 fee.

In 1976 he helped Forest battle their way into the First Division and the following season won league championship and football league cup medals.

The next two seasons he picked up two European Cup winners medals and also another England Cap against Wales. Altogether Larry has made over 400 league appearances ..... and now here he was at Wigan Athletic ..... as the new Manager, and I prepared to step back into the shadows, back to my beloved Reserve team, or to step out altogether if Mr Lloyd wanted to bring in an entire new backroom staff.

However, Larry decided that even though he knew the game inside out, that his ideas were sound, that he was confident in his ability to Manage and Coach, he also felt it necessary to enlist the help of somebody who knew a little about life in the lower divisions so he invited me to become his assistant manager.

I had never considered a life of full-time professional football ever since the game abandoned me when I was young and full of hopes and dreams, now here I was at the age of 37 after being 'kicked into touch' so many times, being offered a position at a fine club like Wigan Athletic that was coveted by some of the big names in the game.

I decided to give myself the chance to put into practice all the things, good and bad that I had picked up during my 'illustrious' career by accepting the position as Larry Lloyd's right hand man ..... only to find that he is left handed!

The only certain thing about football is its uncertainty. I may have been 'Kicked into Touch' by a few good judges of football in my time but I have always retained my genuine love for the game, I never allowed myself to become bitter or resentful and now I was being offered the opportunity of guiding Wigan Athletic and Larry Lloyd into the Third Division for the first time in their history.

I pledged my support to him for one full season and immediately set about signing three solid hard working professionals, who I knew would be the cornerstone of the promotion challenge, together with the good players we had retained from the previous season.

John McMahon a super right back from Crewe was the man I really wanted, I knew him to be just the right sort of character we needed for the job in hand and he came on a free transfer. Clive Evans and Graham Barrow came from Tranmere Rovers and Altrincham respectively and I was delighted with them both and finally Larry persuaded the old warhorse Les Bradd to sign for us from Stockport County and he proved to be just about one of the finest pro's I've ever had the pleasure of working with and his combination up front with Mickey Quinn was simply too much for the Fourth Division to handle and the goals they scored sent Wigan Athletic shooting into Division Three, but, true to form I was no longer with them.

P.S .....

Whoever coined the phrase "Happy as Larry", obviously didn't consult me first, because whilst there obviously were some lighter moments, life as Larry Lloyd's assistant was not one long barrel of laughs, it was like living on Mount Vesuvius ..... and sometimes a little more dangerous!

Our temperaments were a million miles apart and despite trying to convince myself that this mix of total opposites were the very ingredients to make the chemistry work, I knew before the season was barely underway, that I would be on my travels again pretty soon.

I also knew that Larry's influence on the actual pitch was of enormous benefit to the players and there was no doubt in my mind whatsoever, that come the end of the season, Wigan Athletic Football Club would win promotion and that's exactly how things turned out.

Surprisingly my departure from Springfield Park sparked off much interest from the media, with many offers of radio work and from that point, my reputation as an After Dinner Speaker began to gather momentum.

Eventually I received the supreme double accolade for a speaker, when I was invited to propose the toast at The Football Writers Footballer of the Year Dinner, where coincidentally Spike Rawlings my assailant from the Manchester City v Bury game, followed me as the comedian ..... and this time he DID make me laugh!!!!

The PFA Dinner came next, a glittering affair with one thousand three hundred dicky-bowed professional footballers gathered together under the chandeliers of The Grosvenor House Hotel to pay their respects to their own choice of Footballer of the year.

Liverpool and England star John Barnes picked up the award, whilst I was the main speaker and a very happy and proud man I was after such an unforgettable evening ..... but I would have been even happier if John Barnes had been the speaker, and I had been voted The Professional Footballers Association Players Player of the Year ..... but there's still time for that yet!!!!